HIDDEN RICHES

HIDDEN RICHES

*Stories of ACOAs
on the Journey of Recovery*

Paul J. Curtin

CONTINUUM · NEW YORK

1991

The Continuum Publishing Company
370 Lexington Avenue, New York, NY 10017

Printed in the United States of America

Library of Congress Cataloging-in-Publication Data

Curtin, Paul J.
    Hidden riches : stories of ACOAs on the journey of recovery / by
Paul J. Curtin.
        p.   cm.
    ISBN 0-8264-0538-X
    1. Adult children of alcoholics—United States—Case studies.
I. Title.
HV5132.C86   1991
362.29′23—dc20
                                                    91–15443
                                                        CIP

Contents

Author's Note   7

Acknowledgments   9

Introduction   11

1. Self Will Run Riot   15

2. Fighting in New York City   29

3. Fathers and Death   35

4. Sainthood Postponed   41

5. Relationships and Decisions   47

6. More Than Meets the Eye   56

7. Dare I Ask for More?   63

8. I Dare You to Like Me   71

9. Fragility Disguising Rage   81

10. Going Out to Dinner   88

11. Go Away, I Already Gave   94

12. The Graduate   102

Conclusions   111

Hidden Riches in Perspective   118

Author's Note

The identities of the people written about in this book have been carefully disguised in accordance with professional standards of confidentiality and in keeping with their rights to privileged communication with the author.

In order to avoid sexist language the author has used the pronouns he and she interchangeably when not referring to a specific character.

Acknowledgments

Three- and five-year-old boys don't realize authors have a divine right to write. Daniel and Kevin, the terrorist and the bandit, have a peculiar notion it is better to live life than write about it. As a result, this book would never have been finished without the help and support of my wife, Karen. Her insistence that I write and willingness to go "above and beyond" made this possible.

Special thanks go to Wendy Ramsay and Cordis Burns who provide the best administrative and clinical support a person could have.

Finally, I want to acknowledge my gratitude to my parents. They have taught by example that prayers are answered, miracles do happen, and a loving heart perseveres in time.

Introduction

The quickest way to the truth is through a story. This is a book of stories; stories that show adult children of alcoholics (ACOAs) building a foundation of recovery upon their everyday life experiences. School, jobs, marriage, parents, vacations, births, and death all form the tapestry of their recovery. These stories will appeal to a variety of people on many levels. Readers with a personal interest will be able to identify with the individuals whose stories these are. Interested professionals may even find the kernels of a theoretical framework in them. Each story speaks its own language and will be heard in a unique way by each person.

It is not true that the lives of adult children of alcoholics are dull, devoid of emotion, and dramatically free of conflict. Unfortunately, ACOAs are blind to the richness of their lives and are blocked from their emotions. They operate on a sophisticated defensive system that instinctively directs their perceptions and interactions away from painful and unresolved core issues and toward areas of safety, routine, and predictability. They are blind to the vast majority of their inner thoughts, feelings, expectations, and needs. Using a combination of hypervigilence, other-focused insight, and keenly developed intellect, they act defensively in order to maintain a sense of equilibrium. They are **reactors** rather than **actors**. They have no true sense of self.

Living with parents who are active alcoholics forces a child to deny his perceptions, repress his emotions, and close his eyes to the reality and depth of the trauma he is experiencing. This is a natural protective response. The ACOA syndrome develops as these defenses become rigid and entrenched while developmental tasks fail to occur. The child grows into adulthood lacking self-

worth and being unable to see the reality of his life and the depth
of his emotions. As a result, he is forced to act in a defensive
manner. The child protects himself by keeping most people away
and attempting to forestall what he believes to be the inevitable
departure of the few people who are actually close to him.

*"Life is something that happens while ACOAs are waiting to
complete therapy."* Life for the ACOA is gotten through rather
than lived. For the ACOA who is fortunate to find ACOA specific
help, there is a period of excitement. He has finally found something that makes sense out of his life. He enters recovery eager to
grow and happy to have the opportunity to recover. However, as
time goes on, problems arise. The harder the ACOA works at his
recovery, the further away it seems. The more he tries to change
and improve himself, the more pain he feels. The more he drives
himself to act, the more paralyzed he becomes. What began in the
hope of expanding and enriching his life now seems to be con-
fining and restrictive. The ACOA develops an increasing sense of
frustration. His usual methods of self-directed action no longer
work. He intuitively knows that this is going to be different from
anything he has done before. He is being asked to let go of the
very traits he has used to get through childhood and develop at
least some sense of worth.

Instead of giving him life, the recovery process seems to be
taking it away. Things that happen outside of the therapy group
must be supressed so they won't have to be discussed in group.
"Will I have to talk about this?" serves as an external conscience.
"Is this significant enough to bring up?" becomes the standard by
which life's events are measured. The fruitless search for the
magic answer or formula commences. The ACOA desperately
wants to "do it right." Unfortunately, this desperation is matched
by an often unconscious desperation to maintain control of his life
and limit his vulnerability. He does not view recovery as deepening his awareness and acceptance of himself, his relationships,
and his background. He has a primal fear that it will take from him
the very things he has come to rely on and force upon him
perceptions and decisions he is not equipped to handle.

He believes he is being asked to do the impossible and face
too much. He would rather be anywhere else but here and becomes disillusioned with the whole process. *"If this is what
recovery is all about, then forget it!"*

Our friend is missing the point. His anger and fear come from an assault on his self-sufficiency. The ACOA syndrome is like quicksand. The harder one works to overcome it, the deeper one sinks. Throughout the ACOA's life, "hard work," either internal or external, serves to maintain control, dim reality, and numb pain. The AOCA approaches recovery wanting to improve, not to undergo a transformation or conversion experience. He wants to learn to continue doing what is already being done; only better. He is now in a situation in which all of his best efforts only make matters worse. He is seeking external change with minimal internal conversion. His desire to improve himself through his own efforts is the main source of his dilemma. All the recovery process calls for is to see and embrace himself as he is. This is very threatening. He views it as a prescription for disaster, rather than as an invitation to freedom.

ACOAs will recover when they truly want to. Please don't dismiss that statement as a glib phrase or accept it as an unexamined assumption. Do not take it literally to mean that ACOAs who are still struggling lack goodwill and desire. Any talk of recovery entails at least some degree of mysticism. As this book unfolds, and as you open yourself to it, the meaning of recovery will become clear. The book makes use of familiar words to describe an unfamiliar concept. Fortunately, as these stories reveal, there are many familiar things ACOAs can do to put themselves on the path of recovery.

This book examines various life experiences of members of ACOA therapy groups. We find differing versions of common themes; we see ACOAs trivializing their needs and importance while at the same time having an exaggerated fear of others. The themes of "not measuring up" and "not being good enough" appear on a regular basis. ACOAs use morsels of accuracy to protect themselves from the depth of truth. In the vignettes, ACOAs face the dilemma of wanting to share a part of themselves with others, while at the same time being fearful that they will share too much, lose control, and appear weak. They will ask themselves the questions, *"If I am honest with this person I care for, will he get mad and leave me?"*, *"Why won't they leave me alone?"* and *"How can I face this?"* They will be amazed at how often events that they did not deem worthy of discussion are actually emotionally laden. *"I didn't realize there was this much inside of me."*

The most amazing component of these stories is the graced

commitment these ACOAs have to each other. Their struggle to create healthy, intimate relationships in the present will provide the key that will free them from the traumas of the past. They will take risks and break all the rules of alcoholic families. They will express emotions, set limits, make requests, violate "no trespassing" signs, and enter into community with each other. They realize that their recovery will be found in open union with others.

This community of recovery provides a security in which the richness of life can be experienced. Awareness is no longer fundamentally threatening. Fear is present, but it is an expressed and shared fear that actually brings them closer together rather than further apart. Confrontation, shared insights, and different perspectives are no longer viewed as attacks. Instead they are viewed as vital components of the shared journey of recovery.

This book is set in the context of an ACOA therapy group, but applies to any community of ACOAs joining together. Although the incidents discussed will seem familiar to many, the purpose is to invite you to see things differently. Opportunities for recovery are present in each interaction. Hopefully you will look beyond what I am saying to the images of truth I am attempting to capture. I am using simple, fairly commonsense formulas to describe something that is mystical. Understanding will allow you to judge the merits of my theory, but it will not get to where these concepts are pointing.

1
Self Will Run Riot

Kay had reached the point of exhaustion, but she was still compelled to fight and work. She was enormously gifted and talented, excelling at any endeavor she undertook. She was universally regarded as a delight. The only problem was that she didn't believe it. She experienced little, if any, joy or satisfaction in her accomplishments. Her life was a frantic power drive characterized by her attempts to manage, and eventually control, all its aspects.

Kay could no longer maintain her facade of comfortability. What appeared to others as an effortless glide toward mastering the various areas of her life actually exacted a heavy toll on her energy and emotional resources. Kay alone sensed what was at stake. She was not performing and accomplishing based on an internal foundation of security and peace. She was performing and accomplishing in a never-ending quest to develop a sense of self.

The distinction between improving self-worth and creating a sense of self is important. For many people, achievements serve to enhance an already established self worth. That developed self-worth in turn makes continued achievements more rewarding. Kay's accomplishments were different. She was trying to convince others, but mostly herself, that she did have value. She was using external accomplishments to develop an internal identity.

Unfortunately, Kay's lack of self-worth couldn't be repressed any longer. Her self-concept depended on her being perceived as perfect. Being perfect required her to repress the fears and anxieties that were at her emotional core. As these emotions began to slip out, she had to expend more and more energy to maintain her power drive and appearances. Finally she came into treatment with very little energy left. She could not imagine how she could continue to face and deal with her life. She also couldn't conceive of her life being any different. She had reached a figurative state of paralysis. She couldn't go on with her life as it was, but the idea of changing it was too overwhelming for her.

In the beginning, whenever Kay would talk in group she would cry. Her crying was actually sobbing; it was a combination of release and fear. Throughout her life most of her concern and focus was on others. She would talk unceasingly about her parents, sister, husband, and coworkers. Being called upon to focus on and talk about herself was disconcerting. Talking about **herself** and how **she** was doing was something she had yearned for her entire life. At the same time, it scared her so much that she was breathless. In one sense her world was turned upside down. *"What if I get used to this and come to depend on it?" "It's so different from what I'm used to."*

As predictable as her crying was, her apologizing was even more so. She would apologize profusely, wondering how people could stand her when she cried so much. In her mind, sobbing with her face red, nose running, and breath gasping, doomed any relationship she could have with group. To a woman who prided herself on her strength and competence, this was the ultimate weakness. Since she was so weak she thought she wasn't holding up her end of the relationship.

People were very touched by her struggle. Watching her struggle with herself in such an open manner made it impossible for the other members not to be endeared with her. Of course, Kay couldn't believe it. *"Look at me, I'm a mess. How could you possibly like this?"* The other ACOAs told her that they didn't care for her **despite** her being a mess. They cared for her **because** she was such a mess. As you can guess, this brought even more crying from Kay. People actually still cared for her despite her sobbing and losing control of her emotions. She was coming to believe she could let others care for her and not have to perform.

Kay's endearingness and wit were also her main defenses. She had the ability to joke, smile, or delight her way out of most confrontations. These defenses were so good that people rarely had the sense that they were being evaded. That was a true sign of a pro. She also presented in such a manner that people naturally thought she could do no wrong. The conventional wisdom was that her problems stemmed from her having to deal with the inadequacies of others. Whatever problems she had could only be a result of people not doing what they were supposed to do, never from herself. Even though on one level she thought of herself as inadequate, closer to the surface she would commonly condemn others for not living up to her standards. **They** were the problem.

"If this would be different then my troubles would end." "If he would only try harder, I wouldn't have to worry." This "if only . . ." syndrome is very common to children of alcoholic parents. Life generally happens to them. They are continually buffeted by the vagaries of parental alcoholism. The best they can do is "batten down the hatches" and take evasive action. While riding out the storm they hold on to the hope that the external situation will change. "If only they would . . ." (choose from stop drinking, stop fighting, pay attention to me, be like other parents, etc.) then life would be better. Central to this attitude is the core belief that external situations are responsible for internal happiness.

It took people a while before they looked past Kay's pleasant smile and into the content of what she said. They had to get past their delight with her before they could help her. They were able to see that her method of operating necessitated villains. Others were unable to meet her needs. Someone else was always at fault. She believed that she had to work hard to make up for the failings of the people in her life. They simply didn't measure up. As a result she believed she was fundamentally alone. It must be noted that the main cause of this loneliness was herself, not other people. She wasn't able to see that she had systematically shut people out of her life. Her drive to achieve and control left little room for others. Group gave her a chance to become aware of what she was doing.

The main villain in her eyes was her husband, Bob. According to her description, Bob was self-centered and uncaring. His main focus was his work. He had little to do with their child and wasn't supportive of Kay. As a result of this information, he became a resident of the group's doghouse. Eventually, Bob came to a social event at a group member's house. The group members were shocked! First, they never expected this uncaring, unsupportive person to show up, and, second, he wasn't at all like the image Kay had painted. The ogre turned out to be a nice guy.

This became a topic for the next group. The members pointed out that Bob seemed really nice and was great with their son. Kay started to cry and became very upset, not because they liked him, but because they were shocked that they did. She had no idea that she had given them such a negative image of her husband. She truly did love and like him. When she could pause and reflect, she knew he would do anything for her and was a wonderful father. The problem was that she couldn't pause and reflect that often. She would measure Bob against her own frantic, driven standards. The poor man's only crime was that he had a different style than Kay had. Her need for control in this case, both emotional and domestic, shut Bob out of any meaningful sharing or activity. It had to be Kay's way or none at all. When Bob reacted naturally to this pushing away, Kay got angry and resentful. She demanded, *"Why aren't you doing more?"* instead of asking *"Why am I pushing you away?"*

Bob was getting two contradictory messages from Kay. The first was *"I can handle this by myself."* The second was, *"Why aren't you doing your share?"* Nothing he did could completely please her. He was caught between Kay's drive to be perfect and in control and her natural anger and resentment at believing she could rely only on herself. This is a theme that could be traced back to her childhood. Her "superwoman" defense was formed in reaction to the emotional incapacity of her parents caused by alcoholism.

Kay's parents had little nurturing and emotional support to give her. By the time they had spent their resources dealing first with themselves as individuals and then together as spouses, there was nothing left to give to Kay. Kay would try one thing after another to get praise and recognition from her parents. Most of these efforts had at least a flavor of taking care of her parents or fulfilling their responsibilities.

This course of action had an unexpected twist. Each time Kay assumed a caretaker role, she closed the door a little bit on being cared for herself. As her confidence grew, her vulnerability diminished. She became the girl who always did the right thing and didn't need anything. She focused increasingly on what she could **do** while what she **needed** receded into the background.

Her ability to cope and control was a source of great pride, however, that pride covered an anger and an emptiness. She wanted somebody to cope **for** her. She wanted to be in someone's loving control. She wanted to be the recipient of another person's total energies; just like her parents were the focal point of hers. This thought process was also going on at the same time that she believed no one could measure up to her standards. This created an enormous conflict, of which Bob was baring the brunt.

The best way for Kay to keep this conflict beneath the surface was to focus on logistical demands rather than on her own personal needs. She became very goal- and task-oriented. (Her goals and tasks were usually herculean.) What had to be done took precedence over anything else. Of course, *she* would define the task and set the goals. She could not afford to allow her husband to participate in a meaningful manner. Her poor self-concept demanded that she hold the reins. In that way no one would guess she was running scared. In her family of origin she was the organizer, planner, and star by necessity. Alcoholism made sure of that. In her eyes, no one else did what he could or should and as a result was found wanting. She could not depend on anyone. Emotionally she was still living in that alcoholic system.

Bob couldn't be depended on either. Even though he was a good husband and father, he failed the test because Kay's only real goal for Bob was for him to do more. Nothing he could do was right or enough. As long as Kay was stuck in this method of thinking and view of life, she was incapable of being satisfied. There was no way Bob could win because her rules precluded anyone from winning. The "game" was fundamentally flawed. She really didn't want someone to help or assist her. She wanted somebody to take over. At the same time she wanted somebody to take over, she also wanted the person to have the same style, approach, and drive as she did. She wanted someone to continue the course she had set. She was saying, "*I don't want to run things anymore. But here's how you should run them.*"

Kay stood at a turning point. She was frantically trying to keep everything going in order to forestall an imminent collapse. She had no time or energy left over for nurturing either herself or her family. She was blind to the fact that the harder she struggled to be the perfect mother, wife, employee, homemaker, group member, and so on, the more narrow and dark her world became. She was becoming more trapped.

She would claim she was striving so hard in order to make things right for her family. Above all else, she valued her husband and child. Deep down she believed she had to earn that love and maintain a high level of performance in order to keep it. It was inconceivable for her to slow down. *"After all who would want me? What of myself would anyone want?"* She could not see that her drive and perfectionism were separating her from her husband and child. The very things she thought she had to do to keep them were driving them away.

Kay was terrified of being vulnerable and making her **personal** requests and needs known. It was even difficult for her to realize what a personal need is. She was very familiar with *"I need you to clean the grout between the bathroom tiles once a week."* However, *"Please hold me and let me put my head on your chest"* was totally alien. She was much more comfortable arranging and ordering than feeling and needing. The external world must be controlled and arranged because there was so much fear in her internal world. *"If everything is arranged just fine, then I'll be just fine."*

Kay had no sense of external limits. Not being able to do something came from being completely overwhelmed and defeated. She couldn't give a simple no based on her own desire or energy level. She acted as if she were being held accountable by a stern taskmaster, who sneered at any sign of weakness. Life was composed of imperatives and obligations. These imperatives and obligations were generally in conflict and complicated by an increasingly low energy level.

Kay's pregnancy with her second child brought all of this into focus. All of the drives and themes came to a head during the last month of her pregnancy. As you might have guessed, Kay had more to deal with than just being pregnant. There was also her decision to sell her house, move into another, and return to work all within one month of the birth. This sounds like a job for superwoman. Although it was exacerbated by the coming together of major events, this method of operating was not unusual or surprising for Kay.

Kay was feeling alone and trapped. The end of her pregnancy was approaching and she was afraid she wouldn't be able to cope with the delivery and recovery process. She sobbed in group, talking about how she was trying to manage and organize things for her coming stay in the hospital. She expressed great concern about being physically able to cope with a newborn as well as for a two-year-old. In her mind there was no way out. It was only with the group's help that she could see she was viewing this as a solitary project. Even then she could not see any practical alternatives because she had no conception that things could be different. There was a look of shock on her face when somebody suggested that she ask Bob to take a paternity leave. That just wasn't done. The kids were **her** job. She knew immediately that asking him to stay home for a couple of weeks would be enormously significant. She stood at a crossroad.

The legacy of parental alcoholism is the sense that a person is fundamentally on one's own. Alcoholism robs parents of their ability to be consistently nurturing, supportive, and helpful. As a child grows up, she generally takes one of two paths. She could abrogate all personal responsibility and search for someone to latch onto in an attempt to be made complete. She could also assume complete and total responsibility, defensively attempting to control and manage every aspect of her life. This was Kay's path. Both options came from the same root; the basic belief that there is no one to depend on who will be consistently reliable.

Asking Bob to stay home did not go as she had planned. He was thrilled that Kay asked him. Bob, in good faith, had believed she wanted him to go back to work soon after her delivery. Since they never discussed it, Bob thought Kay wanted to be alone with the children so she could bond with them. He also thought that she was worried about the income they would miss if he took time off from his job. He planned on working in order to give her one less thing to worry about. Bob did take a couple of weeks off and loved it. One of the highlights Kay reported was watching Bob's relationship with their oldest child flourish.

It is important to note that Kay did not reject the idea of Bob's helping during this time. Instead it had never occurred to her to ask him for such help. It was outside the realm of her experience. She had no previous role models to have shown her that she did have options. Her power-driven, controlling, franticness actually limited her options and narrowed her visions. All she could see was a never-ending, self-imposed series of tasks. Group helped her put on the brakes and begin to see that she did have alternatives.

With the paternity leave out of the way, there was another crisis to deal with before the baby was born. After Kay left the hospital with her first child, her in-laws came to spend a couple of days with her family. They stayed at her house and Kay was the "hostess with the mostest." She also paid a huge price in terms of a loss of energy and depression. She was dreading this new baby because in her eyes it would automatically mean another influx of relatives. She had nightmares of an indeterminate number of people staying at her house for an indefinite period of time. It would be a "Twilight Zone" of in-laws. Kay alternated between being mad at herself for being such a weakling and at Bob for having such a pushy family. She had done this all in her head. She had accepted the obligation, identified the villains, and tried to conserve her reduced energy in silence.

Kay's attempts at control did not extend to close interpersonal relationships. She believed herself to be a victim with no options. The last thing she wanted to do was to disappoint or make her in-laws angry. She would use all of her resources to manage the agenda they set for her. Compromise, negotiation, setting limits, and making her needs known did not apply to her. She got mad at group when members suggested she could do a number of things to help herself. Among them were not to invite her in-laws, invite them for a specific length of time, have them stay at a hotel and come over at specific times, put them to work in the house, or have them baby-sit. The list was endless. These seemed like simple requests, but they were emotionally charged. Instead of viewing these options as means for protecting herself, Kay viewed them as insulting to Bob's family. In her eyes, to make a request of Bob's family would be tantamount to attacking them.

As a child of alcoholic parents, Kay's key perception was of escalating unreasonable demands made by self-centered people she loved. Alcoholics are generally incapable of mutual exploration of emotional and physical needs resulting in a decision that benefits both parties. To say no to a request is seen as saying no to the entire person. To speak up for oneself and begin to have reasonable expectations upsets the balance that holds the alcoholic family together. In this case, Kay believed that making this reasonable request of Bob and his family would at least alienate her in-laws or at worst threaten her marriage.

Her fellow ACOAs once again provided Kay with a combination of firm advice, an invitation to explore herself, and encouragement to share herself with Bob. She was able to see that her anger at Bob was really anger at herself. She viewed events in the present triggering the anger she had felt throughout her life for having to adjust and accommodate with no consideration for herself.

Saying no, negotiating, and compromising did not have to be a rejection of her husband and his family. These were new concepts that could actually serve to bring the family together in a shared process. In group, her anger at Bob diminished as she focused on her **personal needs** as opposed to her **logistical dilemma.**

Kay was then able to talk to Bob and together they worked out a schedule. The end result was that the visit not only was comfortable but also resulted in the in-laws being put to work. They cleaned and baby-sat, which gave Kay and Bob a chance to be alone. Everyone was happy and everyone benefited from the arrangement. She could not believe they wanted to help her. It was an alien notion to consider that she could be the one people wanted to help and care for. She automatically assumed she had to be the helper and organizer.

It would be too easy if this were the end of the story. Two weeks before the baby was due Kay announced she had sold her home. After they recovered from their shock, the group members pointed out how stressful this act was. Knowing Kay they also said it didn't surprise them. Her next announcement really did surprise them; flabbergasted would be more descriptive of its effect. She said that she and Bob decided to build a new house. The only problem was it wouldn't be ready for five months! Here is the schedule she had set for herself: she would give birth in two weeks, be home with her new child for two weeks, find and move into an apartment during those two weeks, and finally move again in four months when the new house was complete. People in the group were stunned. Rarely had Kay's drivenness been so totally exposed. She had decided all of this on her own. No consideration was given to the toll it would take on her, her husband, her two-year-old child, and the new baby.

Announcement and **alone** are the key words. As the stressors in her life increased, Kay retreated into herself and reverted to a solitary, crisis-oriented, narrow, decision-making process. Dealing with the crisis became paramount to her. This gave rise to her most self-defeating tendencies. She had called upon herself to do too much with too little. She was blind to the damage it caused to herself and her family. Harming her family was the last thing she wanted to do. She would have said that she was working so hard because it helped her family. She couldn't imagine that her attention and anxiety were being assimilated by everyone in the house. In one sense with all good intentions she was replicating the tense atmosphere of her childhood.

Kay eventually came into group with her after-the-fact announcement, which had come after she had analyzed the situation, set her own priorities, and developed a course of action. Her proclamation took the form of *"I have all this to do and I'm scared."* The group's job, in her eyes, was to recognize how hard she was trying and give her support. Of course she wanted to define what support meant. An open decision-making process was not on her agenda. *"Help me carry out my plan"* was the initial tenor of her discussion. If she could have been open, she might have said, *"Here are my thoughts, what do you think is going on? I need your help to set priorities and make a plan."* She wanted help in **carrying out** her decision as opposed to having people help her **make** a decision. She wanted to settle for making an adjustment, whereas a total conversion was necessary.

For Kay, calling time out and saying, *"I can't do it anymore. I need you to help me"* would be admitting defeat. It would also mean being vulnerable and trusting. Such a surrender would threaten her defense of control and competence. She was finding out that she could no longer improve upon a bankrupt method of operating. Yet, at the same time, she was terrified of letting go and taking a leap of faith. She was coming face to face with a decision whether to settle for improvement or in-depth recovery. She had to choose between trying to improve upon her self-directed, self-contained style or taking a step into the unknown of recovery and begin to depend and rely on others.

Kay was torn. Her frantic behavior had developed a momentum of its own. With her pregnancy and worries about the new house she believed she was in the middle of a cyclone. A huge part of her wanted to ride it out, to try to push through one last time. To step off and redefine the situation would be perceived by Kay as failing. The center of her world was her own performance. The needs of the new baby and her family were being ignored. *"How will this affect us as a family?"* was never asked let alone thought about. *"Do we need to be so ambitious and do so much?"* could just as well have been in a foreign language. Peace, calm, and relaxation were viewed as unnecessary luxuries rather than necessary components of a family's adjustment to a new child.

The main difference with regard to this crisis was that Kay was not alone. Being in group gave her a chance to have her franticness interrupted. Group members, being in recovery themselves, had the personal resources to actively intervene in her spiral. They virtually insisted that she stop and step back from the situation. She was unable to pause and freely reflect on her own. The courage and commitment of her fellow ACOAs helped her to slow down and think about a number of things. In particular, she was asked to consider three main points.

1. How her level of stress would effect her baby.
2. The reaction of her two-year-old to the disruption caused by a new baby, being taken from the familiarity of his house, being placed in a strange apartment, and then being moved again in four months.
3. How her marriage would be affected beyond the normal stresses of having a new child as a result of the moving.

Members had to point out to Kay that buying a house and having a new child are two of the most stressful things a family can experience. Kay was trying to do both at the same time, on her own, because she believed it was her obligation to her family. In trying to meet these incredible demands, she was placing herself and her family under a great deal of stress and anxiety.

Kay and Bob finally agreed to buy a house that her family could move into immediately. This reduced the stress and gave the family a sense of stability. Kay had one crisis left. How could she take care of a two-week-old baby and a two-year-old child while packing to move? She was told quite bluntly, *"Hire someone to pack."* Even though she was exhausted physically and emotionally and her family income was over $100,000 a year, she fought the idea. *"Shut up and do it,"* she was told. She did it and actually enjoyed not packing.

The baby was born, the in-laws came and went, and the family moved into a beautiful house. It seemed like a happy ending. However, there was one more crisis left to face. Six weeks after the baby was born, Kay came into group frantic and sad. She was having trouble sleeping, experiencing panic attacks, and felt afraid that she couldn't go on. She was even having trouble at work. *"Work! What work? You never you said you were back at work."* *"Oh, yeah,"* she replied. *"I'm back to work full time."* Many group members began to express anger toward her. They forcefully pointed out a number of things. First of all there was no need for her to go back to work so soon. Her job was assured and available whenever she wanted to go back. There was no pressing financial need. She was reminded that her husband's annual income was over $80,000. What did she prove by returning to work so soon? Since she went back to work full time, there was not one moment when she wasn't upset and frantic worrying how she could do everything she set out to for herself. Even though she was a wreck, Kay continued to add more stress to her life.

One member put it best: *"It's one thing when your insanity screws up only yourself; but when your power-driven need for perfection starts to screw up your baby and kid, that's where I draw the line!"* In her job Kay had counseled hundreds of women about how important a child's first four months were and how it was best for the mother to be at home if at all possible. In her mind, that didn't apply to her. Her grandiosity, which covered her feelings of inadequacy, compelled her to do more. One member best summed up the contradiction between Kay's actions and her values. *"You leave your kids alone at a critical stage so you can go to work and help other mothers give their kids good care."* This hit Kay with a crunching force.

That revelation made the last three months crystal clear to Kay. Going back to work when she had no real need or obligation to go brought everything home to her. It wasn't until the additional stress of work brought such physical discomfort that she was able to experience the cost she was paying. The anger and forcefulness of group members as they supported her, yet advocated for her husband and kids, allowed Kay to see her situation with new eyes. Even Kay could see that her actions did not make any logical sense. The vision was inescapable. She knew deep inside that she had to let go.

Going back to work marked Kay's last-ditch effort to maintain control and have her self-sufficiency remain intact. Going back to work went against everything she believed in regarding her family. Developing this new vision showed Kay in a very vivid manner where she was heading. This realization was also accompanied by an intense catharsis in group. Her outpouring of emotion was not contrived or made to happen on a predetermined schedule. It happened on its own as a logical consequence of finally seeing her life as it was. Once her isolation and pushing her family away became clear, she felt true anguish. Before she only had information about her behavior and its roots, now she could see and feel it.

Kay's story finally came to a happy ending. That night she talked to Bob. Though Bob was a bit taken aback, they decided that Kay would extend her maternity leave. She went in to talk to her boss and was surprised at how understanding and encouraging she was. (Kay still had difficulty realizing what a valuable employee she was and how people would make all sorts of concessions in order to keep her.) Together, she and her supervisor worked out a plan by which she would work one night a week. This would get her out of the house and provide some different stimulation for her. The best part of this arrangement was her supervisor's telling Kay that if she tried to come back again too soon, she would forcibly send her home. People did care for her. Kay discovered that people could be caring when given a chance but they first had to be given a chance.

SUMMARY POINTS

I. ACOAS OFTEN ATTEMPT TO HOLD THEIR FAMILIES TO-GETHER BY MANAGING MOST ASPECTS OF FAMILY LIFE. Though these efforts at control are meant to bring people closer, they actually serve to push them away. Caretaking, when serving as a means of self-definition, causes anger and resentment on both sides.

The ACOA is angry because she can never care enough to produce the desired results. This leaves her with ongoing anger combined with viewing others as ingrates or slackers. The recipients of this "care" are angry because it shuts them out of most aspects of family life. The parts they are allowed into are predetermined and their actions prescribed by the ACOA. Since the recipients can never do enough to meet the ACOA's needs, she often senses frustration and futility.

2. ACOAS' EFFORTS AT HARD WORK AND THEIR SENSE OF RESPONSIBILITY DO NOT REDUCE STRESS IN PERSONAL AND FAMILY RELATIONSHIPS. Their use of self-will and frantic attempts to impose control increase stress and tension. This approach decreases their ability to search for alternatives and narrows their focus. As a result, they approach relationships with little flexibility and fairly rigid methods of interacting.

3. DEVELOPING A NEW VISION IS THE CORNERSTONE OF RECOVERY. Once the reality of an ACOA's life can be seen, embraced, and accepted, recovery **happens**. Rather than enhancing the recovery process, hard work often creates obstacles and barriers. In this instance, once Kay had to stop trying to work on herself and fix her life, she became free to begin her recovery. Once she paused to see the reality of her life situation, awareness occurred and her level of stress was greatly diminished.

2

Fighting in New York City

Ken is wearing his "group face." He is sitting like a statue all rigid and tense. Finally he says *"I want to share with you what happened with me and Evelyn."* He pauses and looks even more serious. *"I'm not sure what it means, but I know I have to talk about it."*

Ken and Evelyn are a young couple who have been dating for four months. This is the first romantic relationship Ken has discussed and processed from the beginning with his ACOA therapy group. The event Ken is referring to occurred during their first weekend trip as a couple. They decided to go to New York City to see some plays and go sightseeing.

While walking around after seeing a play, Ken discovered that he had lost his wallet. Ken and Evelyn were both panic stricken. They began to retrace their steps. Evelyn's frustration turned to anger at Ken. *"How could you!"* *"Why didn't you check your pockets before you left?"* *"What are we going to do now?"* While this tirade was going on, Ken became more cold and detached while his mind raced with possibilities. He came up with the idea that his wallet had fallen out of his pocket while he was watching the play. They raced back to the theater, but it was closed. Unable to get in, Ken decided to report the loss to the police and return to the theater early the next morning. The cab ride back to the hotel was filled with a frosty silence. When they got back to the room, the chill was punctuated with a few more variations of *"I can't believe you lost it"* and a finale of *"It's probably not going to be there."* Ken began to get mad at Evelyn. *"Why doesn't she shut up? I'm doing the best I can. I feel bad enough about loosing it, so I don't need her to rub my nose in it."* All this was thought in silence as Ken stewed in his anger at himself for losing the wallet and at Evelyn for harping on his failure. This served to increase his sense of guilt. In addition to feeling guilty about losing the wallet there was the added guilt about his anger at Evelyn.

The next morning they went back to the theater and discovered the wallet was there. So was the money! The incident, however, had cast a pall, not only over the rest of the trip but throughout the week as well. Ken and Evelyn were unable to process what had happened between them. They were grateful that the anger, guilt, and confusion had lessened in intensity and had receded from their immediate perceptions. They used the technique developed in alcoholic families of waiting for the conflict to subside, letting the emotions wane away, and then proceeding as if nothing had happened. Unfortunately, since Ken was in an ACOA group, he was unable to ignore the aftertaste of the incident.

As he relates this, it is clear that Ken is struggling to force himself to talk. He had previously attempted to ignore or lessen the significance of the argument. Now that he was ready to talk about it with his peers, he swung to the other end of the spectrum and gave it monumental importance. As a result he presents in a manner that is very formal, factual, and controlled. This is because Ken has two major fears. The first is that this incident showed he was incapable of having a healthy romantic relationship. The second fear is that he viewed his fellow ACOAs as combined jurors and executioners, waiting to declare him guilty of romantic incompetence and sentence him to a life of loneliness.

He fears that this blowup is symptomatic of a fundamental flaw in his relationship with Evelyn. He wonders how he could be attracted to someone who would react the way she did. He also worries that she may be right after all and he really is careless and thoughtless. He had wanted to comfort her but had gotten lost in his own thoughts and fears. Getting angry at her served to further his doubts about himself. He can see no way of things ever getting better.

Coming from an alcoholic family makes it difficult for Ken to trust and develop a sense of community. Ken is now afraid of the ACOA group. In times of stress old defenses arise, and he views them as "people who will judge me harshly" and "people who will take away my pleasure." Filled with confusion, conflict, and fear, he does not view his fellow ACOAs as individuals who have unconditional care for him. They become a monolithic entity he has to maneuver around in a protected and controlled manner. He tries to give them the most information with the least amount of revelation. He does not want them to confirm his own belief that he is a failure.

Ken is stuck. He believes that if he explores what happened it will reveal that not only is this relationship bad, but he is also doomed to **never** having a healthy, romantic relationship. Even worse, if he explores it with group, they will order him to break up with Evelyn and demand that he never go out with anyone again. This is why he is so serious and tense. However, all is not lost. By even beginning to discuss this, no matter how controlled, he is violating all the rules of alcoholic families. Even though he is controlled, guarded, and full of self-censorship, he is taking a leap of faith in community with others.

His fellow ACOAs now give him a great gift. They don't treat what happened seriously! In fact, some are struggling not to smile too obviously. Finally, someone says to Ken, *"What would you really have liked to say to Evelyn when she was bitching at you?"* Ken is apprehensive. *"What do you mean?"* *"Well, you must have been mad. What would you have liked to tell her?"* Ken replies, *"I wish I could have said 'I think you're being unfair.' "* Now the group starts to get excited and people start to kid him about his response. Ken begins to smile. He admits he really wanted to yell at her, tell her to get off his back, throw her out of the cab, and even shove a knish in her face! He starts to relax and once he is relaxed, he tells about all the "rotten" thoughts he's had about Evelyn since the weekend. He had built up a twin monster of self-righteousness and despair that is now being released through the invitation of others.

Ken did not realize that his feelings of anger and desire to throw Evelyn out of the cab were normal and perfectly human. (As were Evelyn's.) As an ACOA he has had no ongoing example of the cycles of conflict, resolution, and continued growth. He had to repress and censor his emotions and thoughts because of the mistaken notion that they represented a fatal flaw both in himself and in the relationship. In fact, not only are these emotions normal, they are universal in our society. That is why people were able to invite him to be real and why his realness, in turn, invited the other group members to relate similar experiences.

Ken learned that couples tend to have fights during periods of high stress. He saw that the trip was an explosion waiting to happen. It was their first weekend sojourn; they were in a strange city, with tons of stimulation; and, most touching, they were both desperately trying to make the weekend wonderful for each other. Of course there was going to be a fight.

The key to Ken's recovery is that as he shared with others, he was able to laugh about the incident rather than defend it.

When Ken was able to accept his humanness and join in community with others, he began to relax. His view of his fellow ACOAs changed. They were no longer a board of judges predisposed to point out his failures. Instead, they were a community of his peers with the same background, all having similar experiences. This blowup, which he initially believed branded him as inferior and separate, actually provided a common ground for him and the group. It became a celebration of being human rather than an exposition of failure.

SUMMARY POINTS

1. ACOAS MAY TEND TO VIEW GROUP MEMBERS IN AN ADVERSARIAL MANNER. In this case Ken viewed the group members as people who would judge him harshly and people who wanted to take from him the little pleasure he did have. This had its root in his relationship with his alcoholic parents. The darkness of alcoholism did not permit much pleasure. If Ken exhibited too much happiness or excitement, he would very quickly be chastised. Ongoing happiness for one member only highlighted the gloom of the other members. Pleasure was obtained despite the family situation.

Since they transfer their experiences with their families of origin onto the group, ACOAs need help exploring the benefits gained by sharing in a community. Having no experience of a shared open process based on mutual support, they find it difficult to imagine that group would be different from their families. The key is to be able to view group members as people who want to give freedom, rather than take it away.

2. DISCUSSION OF ROMANTIC RELATIONSHIPS IN ACOA THERAPY GROUPS ARE INITIALLY GUARDED IN AN EFFORT TO PROTECT PERCEIVED FAILINGS. Romantic relationships are often used as a measure of self-worth and self-definition. *"At least one person thinks I'm special."* ACOAs tend to cling to romantic relationships because "something" is better than nothing. There is also a sense that they may never get another chance to have one. There is a belief that to admit to problems in a relationship is to acknowledge that it must end. They find it difficult to view relationships as dynamic rather than static, and evolving as two people grow.

3. BEING RAISED BY ACTIVE ALCOHOLICS DOES NOT GIVE A PERSON A BELIEF THAT CONFLICT CAN LEAD TO GROWTH IN A RELATIONSHIP. Alcoholism is the central organizing factor in alcoholic families. It is the root of most conflict in alcoholic families, yet it is rarely addressed consistently and productively. Conflict must be suppressed or diverted from the alcoholism or else radical changes would become necessary. Since growth is unlikely, if not impossible, in families with active alcoholism, conflict only increases the pain and trauma. It does not lead to improvement. In fact, conflict involving alcohol often leads to emotional or physical violence. Conflict is to be avoided because it only leads to dangerously unpredictable outcomes.

4. ACOAS TEND TO BE INTERNALLY FOCUSED AND SERIOUS. They need the invitation of others to realize that they are not alone and that most problems are not catastrophes. As children the weight of the world was on their shoulders. They viewed through their self-centered eyes the major tragic forces of alcoholism at work in their families. They vacillated between thinking they are to blame to thinking they are responsible for fixing the family. At the same time there was usually nobody to provide them with support and nurturance. This created an exaggerated sense of self-importance and seriousness. (It is necessary to note that some ACOAs respond by acting totally irresponsible, but it has the same root as being super-responsible.) Being in community with others allows ACOAs to realize that they do not have as

much control over their lives as they would imagine and that life tends to go on despite their best efforts.

5. THE ISOLATION OF FAMILY ALCOHOLISM FORCES A SENSE OF UNIQUENESS THAT THE GROUP PROCESS IS PARTICULARLY WELL SUITED TO ADDRESS. Many ACOAs have a terminal case of humanness that they try to deny. By watching others share their lives they begin to see they are not alone. The bond of an ACOA group is vulnerability and shared experience as opposed to strength and lack of problems.

Ken was able to see he was not alone. His fight with Evelyn turned out to be a rite of passage every couple has to experience. He thought that sharing his New York adventure would set him apart as a failure. In reality, exposing his problems cemented his bond with the group members and gave him hope for his relationship with Evelyn.

6. ACOAS ARE OFTEN BLIND TO THE VARIOUS SITUATIONAL STRESSORS THEY EXPERIENCE. Chaos and unpredictability are the cornerstones of alcoholic families. As children it was necessary to deny the reality of the day-to-day tension they experience. Many become quite adept at functioning in a crisis. It's as if they were trained to act rather than feel. However, repression and denial eventually take their toll.

Ken had no idea that this first romantic getaway was stressful. He thought that because he cared for Evelyn the weekend should go perfectly. If it didn't then it meant the relationship was bad. Once the conflict occurred, he attributed it to character defects rather than situational realities. It became very serious. The group helped him to see how natural his feelings were. This gave him a sense of perspective, which led to acceptance. When combined, they eventually led to Ken's developing a sense of humor.

3

Fathers and Death

Tom wanted to report something. An uncle had recently died and Tom had gone to the funeral. He said that it was difficult for him to go but he was glad he did even though it was painful. He wanted to leave it at that and let the group move on. His intention was merely to inform. Luckily the group pressed him to fill out the story. He disclosed that his mother would periodically leave his alcoholic father and take the kids with her. She would take them to this uncle's house, and he would take care of them for a couple of months. (After a number of years in group, this is the first time Tom ever revealed either of these major facts.) This uncle was very significant to Tom because he was a father figure who actually tried to create a sense of family for him.

The group members appeared more moved by the story than Tom did. He wanted to focus on how glad he was to be able to do the right thing and go to the funeral. They wanted him to share more about the previously unrevealed traumas and what his uncle meant to him. Group was at an impasse. Just before they began to badger Tom to try to force him to touch the sadness he had spent a lifetime supressing, Susan spoke.

Her father had recently died and she was discovering as time passed her anger toward him increased. Her father had a stroke a year before he died. It didn't incapacitate him, but it required ongoing doctor's care as well as bed rest and caution. Her anger stemmed from the fact that her father wouldn't follow the doctor's plan. *"God Damn it! He just kept getting out of bed."* Her father would often not take his medicine, miss doctor's appointments, and overexert himself. As a result, instead of undergoing a gradual rehabilitation and regaining health, he was dead within a year. *"I hate him for doing this to himself and to me, but I love him so much and miss him so badly."*

A change happened while Susan was talking. When Tom spoke everyone was focused on him and was ready to "help" him process his loss. As Susan spoke, they began to look into themselves and into their own relationships with their fathers. This is not to say that they were not profoundly connected with Susan. The richness of her sharing and the depth of her openness forged a bond between them. Her vulnerability also invited the others to look at their own pain regarding their fathers.

Sam next shared that he still hadn't gotten over his father's death even though it had been ten years since he had died. He told how his father developed lung cancer from cigarette smoking. It was excruciating for him to watch his father continue to smoke. Each time his father lit a cigarette Sam wanted to yell, *"Can't you see you're killing yourself?"* Once he even said, *"I need a father! I don't want you to die!"* Eventually the cancer progressed and became inoperable. For the first time Sam told group what happened the night his father died. He went to the hospital room to tell his father he loved him and to say good-bye. He wanted to tell his father how much he meant to him and to thank him for everything. His father would have none of it. Each time Sam tried to talk, his father would stop him. Eventually he threw him out of the room saying *"I'm tired and don't want to talk. Just leave me alone and come back later."* Those were the last words he said to Sam. His father died that night.

John then talked about his father. John's relationship with his father had been formal and distant most of his life. That changed when his father had a heart attack. After the attack he began to seek out John. His father wanted to be around John, but he didn't want to talk. John wanted to pour his heart out to his father but didn't know how to begin. They would go for long walks with few words passing between them. They were spending more time together than ever, yet John felt more estranged. He thought his father didn't love him because he wouldn't talk to him. Finally, his father had a stroke and died soon afterward. At first John could only focus on the anger he felt. Others pointed out that they would have given anything to have had the relationship with their father that John did. By acknowledging the anger, John became free to embrace the tenderness he also felt. He was able to admit that he considered that time spent with his father as very special. His anger served to protect him from the pain. Until he acknowledged that pain he was unable to experience the warmth he felt.

Judy was afraid to talk because she felt out of sync with the group. *"I'm happy my father isn't alive,"* she declared. *"He was mean and beat me when he was alive. When he died, I said 'I'm glad it's over.' "* The other members were taken aback by the certainty and finality of her pronouncement. They gently pointed out that there had to be more feelings inside of her. No matter how badly a child is mistreated that yearning to be loved by a parent has to be present in some form or another.

Judy had blocked out any sense of yearning and love for her father with an almost impermeable, insistent anger; yet, at the group's invitation, she began to soften. *"Well, my father did throw me a curve before he died."* She revealed that her father was dying when she was expecting her first child. When she would visit him he would cry and sob because he would be dead before his grandchild was born. This created a painful conflict in her that had three dimensions. The first was, *"My kid will be lucky not to have you around."* The second was, *"Every kid should have a grandfather. With the pressure off, he might make a good grandfather."* Most painful was the third—*"Why couldn't he feel this way about me?"* Judy realized at some level that if that third dimension broke through it would threaten her entire defensive structure. That is why she struggled to maintain control.

Finally, Dan, who had been silent and rigid the whole group, spoke. *"This has been so hard for me to relate to since both my parents are still alive."* The group was so stunned that they completely ignored him. His silent, isolating defenses set up the following reasoning: **This is about dead fathers. My father is still alive. Therefore it doesn't concern me.** He could therefore retreat into himself until the topic was switched. It would be too painful to realize that his alcoholic father is removed from him even though he's still alive.

What's wrong with this picture? What is missing from all of this? **There has been absolutely no mention of alcoholism!** The absence of any reference to alcoholism speaks volumes. This is an ACOA therapy group, but no one mentioned alcoholism. All of these fathers were alcoholics, yet no one made the connection between their alcoholism and their deaths. In a very real sense alcoholism and the resulting personality patterns either caused their fathers deaths or increased the pain of those deaths.

If Tom's father wasn't an alcoholic, he would not have elevated his uncle to such a significant position. If Susan's father wasn't drinking, he probably would have followed the doctor's plan. The guilt caused by Sam's father's alcoholism prohibited him from talking with Sam and looking back on his life with him. The isolation and fear that alcoholism imposed on John's father prevented him from being able to reach out to John. Alcoholism caused the self-loathing her father projected onto Judy and his drunkenness promoted the violence. **Yet as these situations were discussed, alcoholism was never considered.**

It became clear that these ACOAs had spent much of their lives reacting to their relationship with their alcoholic fathers. Tom continues to try to make good and earn his keep in order to forestall rejection and the revelation of his worthlessness. Susan is very controlling and constantly attempting to manage the lives of her husband and son for their own good. Sam acts like an authoritarian boss, husband, and father needing no one and expecting people to follow his "orders" unquestionably. John has strained relationships with his supervisors. He overworks and tries to impress them, yet he is continually angry because they don't give him the recognition and acknowledgment he deserves.

This universal yearning to be loved by parents is often too painful for ACOAs to acknowledge. This feeling gets transformed into guilt for not doing enough to save or reach out to their parents. It can be disguised as anger over their parents' failure to meet their needs. Denial can repress the fact that they have deep feelings toward their parents. Often they are overly compassionate regarding their parents' plight. Pity regarding the tragedy of their parents' lives makes their own lives less tragic. They can then rise above the situation.

The way the group worked is significant. Tom's story primed the pump for others even though he was unable to fully benefit from it. The group showed maturity and health by not going after Tom. They could have easily spent the entire session fighting with him, trying to get him to do what he didn't have the ego strength to do. Instead, people allowed it to trigger and release things inside of themselves that they needed to share. In an ACOA group once the defenses of the shadow world of true emotion are breached, a critical mass of sharing and bonding often occurs. Vulnerable self-revelation creates a powerful atmosphere of acceptance. That atmosphere of acceptance in turn allows others to share just as deeply. The tenderness group members felt for each other allowed them to be tender with themselves. Acceptance by the group allows an ACOA to accept the reality of his life and his feelings.

What about Dan and the other members who sat in silence? That silence indicated the severity of impairment and the severity of the ACOA syndrome. The session had been extremely threatening to them. It dealt with one of the most painful areas they encounter. They remained silent, attempting to appear as if they hadn't been affected. **Internally, no one is neutral on this subject.** A major battle was occurring inside each of them, of which they only had a vague inkling. Even though they were silent, it was critical that they be addressed and reassured. Their silence was not an indication of lack of feelings or of failure. It merely meant they were not yet ready to look that deep into themselves. Acknowledging their struggle and affirming their worth to the group increases the chance that they will continue the process and share more the next time. Everyone did all they were capable of doing.

SUMMARY POINTS

1. ACOAS GENERALLY HAVE REVERSED ROLES WITH THEIR PARENTS. This is always true on an emotional level and usually on a practical level as well. Their reaction to parental alcoholism was that they came to regard themselves as caretakers while being blind to their own needs. The idea that parents are supposed to create an environment that is child focused did not develop. Everything revolved around the alcoholism and the hold it had on the parents. As a result, the children became adept at responding to the needs of others, yet maintained an internal self-reliance.

2. WHETHER THEIR PARENTS ARE ALIVE OR DEAD, HOW ACOAS RELATE TO THEM IS OF GREAT IMPORTANCE. This cannot be stressed too much. Developmental tasks, personality formation, and ego structure are all affected by parental alcoholism. Alcoholism results in skewing and incompleteness in the basic parent-child relationship. This carries over into most relationships that ACOAs have as they unconsciously try to resolve that fundamental conflict.

3. ACOAS TEND TO MAKE THEIR PARENTS AND THEIR RELA-
TIONSHIP WITH THEM ONE-DIMENSIONAL. For example,
they tend to minimize pain by reducing parental alcoholism
to acts of drinking. *"My Mom was great unless she was
drunk."* Parents are described as all good or all bad. If
ACOAs can narrowly focus on one aspect of their parents,
then the pain is reduced. It is easy to be angry at your
parents and claim to have absolutely no expectations of
them. Actually ACOAs do have expectations, hopes, and
yearnings but they are too painful to acknowledge. Being
angry or disgusted shuts the door on that pain. As ACOAs
develop the strength and security to explore their relationships with their parents, they discover that these relationships are actually quite complex. Being able to explore
the richness of their emotions allows them to view their
parents with reality and compassion. **Since they no longer
have to defend against these feelings, they become free to see
how they are present in most of their other relationships.**

4. EXPLORING THEIR RELATIONSHIP WITH THEIR PARENTS IS
EXTREMELY THREATENING TO SOME ACOAS. Even after a
number of years in group some members will not have the
ego strength to explore this area. Many ACOAs have been
damaged and scarred deeply. It is important to not push
them in this area. It is just as important to affirm them so
that they do not view themselves as failures. For some the
affirmation they get, even though they can't explore this area
at a particular point, is more useful than the actual exploration. It sets the stage for the possibility of further growth.

5. ACOAS OFTEN PREFER TO FOCUS ON DOING WORK FOR
OTHERS. In Tom's case members attempted to focus on him.
They wanted to work for him. The discussion was turning
into a game of Twenty Questions. There was an overall sense
of discomfort, but people felt obliged to help him. Susan
established a direct connection with their hearts rather than
their heads. Her openness provided an invitation for them to
share themselves. It set the tone for self-revelation. Tom and
Susan demonstrated opposite ends of the continuum.

4

Sainthood Postponed

Denise came to her ACOA group extremely upset. Very teary, she reported she was angry, frustrated, and having difficulty sleeping. She had also experienced a loss of energy and a mild depression. Three weeks earlier a "relative" was in a terrible car accident and had been in a coma ever since. Denise believed her sorrow and anger regarding the accident were the source of her distress.

She explained how she had gone to the hospital every day for the last three weeks. She would spend a half hour sitting quietly in the hospital room trying to pray, but being somewhat distracted. She felt badly that she was powerless to help the person in the coma. At this point, a group member interrupted and asked her who the "relative" was. Denise had been so intent on talking, she forgot to be specific. It turned out that this "relative" is actually her husband's brother's fiancée! *"Isn't that the one you can't stand?"* laughed a couple of group members. With a shy smile Denise said "yes." *"Isn't she the one you were furious with for planning her wedding on Christmas Eve?"* Looking like she had gotten her hand caught in the cookie jar, she acknowledged that also. She went on to say that she had angry thoughts about the both of them and had no particular feelings of closeness toward her future sister-in-law once removed. At this point the group became animated and almost giddy. *"You seem to be intent on setting the world record for visiting a person you don't like who's in a coma!"*

Denise was becoming visibly more relieved. Trying not to laugh, she blurted out, *"I'm the only one other than the parents who visit every day. In fact the other day they said I was a saint!"* At this point the whole group was laughing with Denise leading the way. A couple of members tried to become serious (i.e., grim) because they thought it was inappropriate to treat anything lightly, but they were fighting a losing battle. Members started to make offers: *"If you want, I'll go for you since she won't know the difference." "Would you mind visiting my ex-husband's step-child's half brother who's sick?"* The sadness and depression were lifted from Denise immediately. She had experienced a transformation regarding these issues.

What was going on? A number of things were evident as the ACOA group finished laughing and reviewed what had happened. The accident triggered a primitive sense of self-centered guilt in Denise. On a deep level there was a sense that her hostility and anger toward this person caused the accident. Now that this tragedy had occurred she had to atone by keeping a vigil at the hospital. This is very similar to the self-centered view of young children of alcoholics. They believe they cause their parents to drink; that their parents get drunk because the kids have done something wrong; and that they should have the resources to alleviate their parents' alcoholism.

Denise's feelings of guilt were transformed into an over-developed sense of concern and responsibility. As a result, she went to extraordinary lengths to assuage them. This was not a conscious process. It never occurred to her to ask, "Why am I doing this?" She just reacted instinctively. It is important to note that she did not bring this up in group until the third session after the accident occurred. She did not believe it was worth discussing and could not see what talking about it would accomplish. In her mind it was simply doing what was necessary. When she finally was able to talk, it was not about the visiting. Instead, she talked about her feeling of anger toward a God who would let such a terrible thing happen, and her frustration and depression regarding such a young person in a coma.

Her fellow ACOAs allowed her to examine the whole premise behind her visits. They pointed out that she was going to extraordinary lengths to do more than the situation required. She was asked to explore the feelings she was experiencing and why she felt compelled to visit the hospital. They pointed out that her use of the term "relative" wasn't quite accurate. Most importantly, they invited her to explore how she really felt about this woman.

They also reminded her that sainthood is not a requirement for membership in the ACOA group. This gave her a sense of freedom. She was able to see that she was spending an hour each day going to a hospital to visit a person she didn't really know or like. She was spending all this time and effort visiting someone who was in a coma and had no awareness of her presence. No wonder she was angry, frustrated, and depressed! She was doing something she didn't want to do out of a misplaced sense of atonement and obligation. Yet it never occurred to Denise that this was the basis for her depression.

This is another example of how the acceptance by other ACOAs in a group setting allows a person to accept herself. ACOAs are well versed in presenting "proper" appearances to hide a different (less acceptable to them) internal reality. One member shared that she drove fifty miles each day to visit her husband's sick mother (who she also wasn't particularly fond of) while her husband stayed home. Others shared how they took care of distant relatives at the expense of their own families. Another told of spending so much time helping others at work, he couldn't pursue his own projects and therefore missed a promotion he thought he deserved. Denise's deep dark secret about her true feelings and her unconscious compensation for them did not make her an outcast. Being open about them not only made her feel relieved and closer to others but also showed her how she was the same as others after all.

Denise had one more fear she had to deal with, namely, *"How am I going to stop visiting and have no one notice?"* The woman in the coma wouldn't notice, but her parents presented a problem. Denise had built herself up to be a combination of Florence Nightingale and Veronica of the Veil. She thought it would be a crushing blow to the woman's parents if she didn't continue her daily visits.

This is not surprising for someone from an alcoholic family. Parental alcoholism causes a child to develop an exaggerated and warped sense of importance and responsibility. A child often believes she is alone and everything depends upon her. With her parents incapacitated by alcoholism, a child must develop a rigid sense of control. *"If I don't do it, no one will."* (In the least, alcoholics are incapacitated emotionally and are unable to provide nurturance and emotional support for their children. Quite often they are incapacitated in a practical sense as well, leaving many household responsibilities to their children.)

Lacking an internal sense of self-love an ACOA believes that worth equals performance. Mistakes become more than errors. They become a devaluation of self. Doing for others and being of use to others shows that an individual has value and is worthy of notice. Denise was in a dilemma. She was caught between thinking *"What kind of person would stop visiting a sick person?"* and *"What will her parents think if I do stop?"*

Once again the community of ACOAs is crucial. It provides a different perspective to counter such unrealistic thinking. It also provides a foundation of safety, care, and acceptance that allows her to take risks and break old patterns. *"It doesn't matter what happens, we'll be here for you."* They gave her the awareness to acknowledge that she wanted the parents to view her as a "saint" as well as the resources to resign that job. These were totally unexpected gifts for Denise. At the beginning, she truly believed there was nothing to talk about. It never occurred to her that she had options. She only said something in group because she wanted to let people know what was going on. **She never thought group could give her freedom, because she didn't realize she wasn't free to begin with.**

Now that the decision was made, Denise's first instinct was just to stop going to the hospital. ACOAs often prefer to just slip away, rather than to acknowledge and embrace the pain of separation. Making a conscious, informed decision to alter or end a relationship and then communicating that decision goes against the pattern of alcoholic families. Many family members bide their time and wait to slip away. To acknowledge and explore the reasons for leaving would eventually lead to addressing the alcoholism. That is to be avoided at all costs. With the group's support, Denise was able to do it in a straightforward manner. She went to the hospital and told the girl's parents she was not able to keep up her schedule of visits. (She had to resist the desire to tell them her whole life history and the various reasons for her decision.) They were very gracious and grateful and told her how they would always appreciate what she had done. It was nothing like she thought it would be. The earth didn't open under her feet, bells and whistles didn't sound, and the girl's parents didn't wail or gnash their teeth. The only thing that happened was that Denise was a bit freer and a bit closer to recovery.

SUMMARY POINTS

1. ACOAS TEND TO HAVE A SELF-CENTERED FOCUS THAT EXAGGERATES THEIR SENSE OF RESPONSIBILITY. Many are still in a primitive developmental stage in which they equate their thoughts with reality. This is one of the reasons they engage in self-censorship. *"If this anger gets out, I'm afraid I'll hurt someone."* Stray thoughts are given the same weight as considered judgments. They are afraid that revealing "nasty thoughts" would place them outside the pale of decent society. In this case, Denise could not tolerate being angry at a person who had a tragic accident and went to great lengths to put things right.

2. ACOAS OFTEN BECOME SO WRAPPED UP IN AN ONGOING PROBLEM THEY CEASE TO VIEW IT AS A PROBLEM AND IN-STEAD SEE IT AS A CONDITION OF EXISTENCE. Many times ACOAs do not talk about the very things they need to talk about. This is often not a deliberate decision. It also does not occur to them to view it as worthy of consideration. In alcoholic families, members develop a "what's the use" mentality. Things are discussed or actions taken to reach a specific obtainable goal. The idea of sharing one's life with others and inviting them to share in return is alien. Many emotions regarding hurt feelings and unmet needs are re-pressed because expressing them won't change anything.

3. IN ACOA GROUPS PROBLEM SOLVING CAN IMPEDE THE PROCESS OF SELF-REVELATION. This is because the problem initially identified is usually not the root problem. The pro-cess of exploration is more important than finding a correct solution. The group could have given Denise a visitation schedule in five minutes, but the richness of discovery and sharing would have been lost. Instead of only having a re-duction of stress, Denise had developed a valuable awareness. She could see how the theme of overrespon-sibility and needing to be viewed as deeply caring was at

work in other areas of her life. Problem solving would only have channeled that drive into another area. Since Denise had the courage to actually explore the roots of her behavior, it had a chance to dissipate.

4. ACOAS OFTEN USE PROPER APPEARANCE TO HIDE AN UN-ACCEPTABLE INTERNAL REALITY. Denise's operating was based on *"If I visit a lot no one would guess I had such mean thoughts."* This too can be traced back to alcoholic families. If the family looks good enough, no one will know that alcoholism is present. Of course, this facade eventually collapses and people have to work harder and harder to compensate for the internal emptiness. Eventually families get so removed from themselves that they have no sense of who they are.

5. LAUGHTER IS ESSENTIAL TO RECOVERY. Being serious can be counterproductive. When the group started to laugh at Denise's trying to impress somebody in a coma she felt relief. What was a grim, self-determined task, changed into something that was quite outrageous and universal for ACOAs. She was invited, rather than forced, to see how she was overreacting. Denise was connected enough to see that the group was not laughing at her. The laughter showed that it was who she was, not what she did, that they valued.

5

Relationships and Decisions

ACOA therapy groups involve more than attending group one night a week. The relationships people are called to make extend beyond the group session. This results in a variety of emotions, opportunities, obstacles, and possibilities for ACOAs. The complexity of developing healthy, intimate relationships with each other, both in and out of group, reveals many of the scars, themes, and perceptions developed in response to being raised by active alcoholics. Members of an ACOA group have much in common, but also have a wide variety of personalities and interests. Accepting and acknowledging this diversity is part of the recovery process, but it is also a source of tension and conflict.

The complexity and multilevels of relating became clear one night in an ACOA group. The group was composed of people who had been in group for various lengths of time, ranging from four years to four months. Two issues arose that session. The first was that Laura and Nellie were talking about buying a house together. Second, a fairly new member, Joel, was claiming that members were trying to brainwash him and force him to have dinner with them after group. How these two seemingly different areas were processed was very revealing. It showed ACOAs striving and struggling to relate and be honest with each other. It also showed how they attempted to identify the defensive postures they have had to develop and the difficulty encountered in attempting to let them go.

Laura and Nellie had been in group together for over three years. They had been talking in group for a couple of weeks about buying a house together. Most of their thoughts were positive, and the rest of group was generally supportive. Finally, they told group that they had decided to buy a two-family house and had made an appointment with a real estate agent. At this point something changed. Group members had been both supressing thoughts that were not optimistic and also not saying "silly" thoughts that came to mind. Now that this house hunt had become real, they were burdened with the struggle between being honest and being supportive. It's important to note that the ACOAs had a tendency to believe that honesty and supportiveness were mutually exclusive.

Nellie was first to start. She was embarrassed to admit that she was jealous because Laura had a boyfriend and she did not. She was afraid that seeing Laura and her boyfriend on a regular basis would exacerbate the pain she felt about not dating. Laura, for her part, was jealous of Nellie because she had a lot more money for a down payment on the house and would be able to spend more to fix things up and decorate her apartment. Both of these "dark thoughts" were perfectly innocent and natural, yet both Laura and Nellie were afraid to acknowledge them. They were afraid the other person would get angry and call off the deal. As a result, their interactions became more guarded while they both tried to generate enthusiam and optimism.

Their openness invited the others to speak. Martha said that she was afraid the two of them would get closer and she would be left out. Joanne was concerned because she couldn't figure out how visiting would work. If she came over to visit Nellie, would Laura feel left out if she didn't stop by her place also? Sue was sad because seeing Laura and Nellie doing something together made her realize how lonely her life had been and how she wished she could have done a project with a friend.

It was Pete who named the universal fear by saying, *"If you guys get into a big conflict over the house it might break up the group."* Nellie too shared this fear. She knew she had a tendency to demand that people support her. If there was a fight between her and Laura, she was fearful she would revert back to her old tendency of getting people to take her side against someone else. Other members said they were afraid about having to choose between Laura and Nellie if a conflict arose.

Conflict in alcoholic families is usually a "zero sum game." There has to be an ultimate loser or villain and an ultimate winner or hero. The object is to destroy the other person, as opposed to working together to find the truth. The reason for this is that if the conflict is pursued honestly in an attempt at resolution, it would inevitably point back to the alcoholism. That is unacceptable. Instead, conflict becomes poisoned. It is supressed with a seething sense of self-righteousness for oneself and disgust toward the villain. If it is unleashed, it flares up in a well-aimed strike for the jugular leaving the loser totally demolished.

As members talked, they came to see that conflict and difference are normal and natural. Not only could such conflicts be resolved, but they could also result in growth. Group members realized that they would not have to choose between Nellie and Laura. They also realized that they would not have to shun or avoid them when conflict did arise. Rather than taking sides, they could make a commitment to both of them. Their fellow ACOAs were vital to Laura and Nellie. By affirming and reassuring both of them, group provided a forum for addressing conflict and a community to help in its resolution. **There is a vast difference between resolving a conflict and winning a fight.**

Some members felt a bit sheepish admitting that they were jealous of Laura and Nellie or that they were afraid of being left out. They were very harsh toward themselves. *"Don't be such a baby"* could best describe this notion. Feelings of abandonment and being left out are sensitive areas for children of alcoholics. Parental alcoholism resulted in their being abandoned by, or left out of the world of, the most significant people in their lives, their parents. Repression, empathetic understanding, and feigned indifference are some of the most common responses. Unfortunately, this produces long-lasting scars that color most intimate relationships of the majority of ACOAs.

Expressing these so-called baby or weakling type thoughts is actually an act of strength. It is being honest about a very real emotion. It is not pandering, pleading, or being a crybaby. It is being appropriately honest in order to get past these thoughts and expand a relationship. In ACOA groups these thoughts are almost universal. By acknowledging them, members reduce the power of these thoughts, establish a sense of commonality, and become free to be fully present for each other.

Laura and Nellie's situation leads us into an interesting area. How do unequal relationships affect the ACOA therapy group? During the course of a member's time in group, he will be attracted to some people more than to others. There will be many groupings based on mutual interests. Our ACOA therapy groups are different from more traditional groups in that members are strongly encouraged to socialize and interact outside of group. As a result, unequal relationships, social dilemmas, and feelings of belonging and being left out often arise. The therapy group is not the primary vehicle for an ACOA's recovery. It plays an important part, but it exists in conjunction with intensive involvement with the twelve-step programs, such as Alcoholics Anonymous and Al-Anon. ACOAs take the concept of fellowship, "telephone therapy," helping each other, and social activities learned in the twelve-step programs and apply them with a fervor to their group. As a result, the weekly therapy sessions are only one part of the weekly "group-centered" activity.

In addition to providing wonderful opportunities, group presents problems as well. The situation with Joel provides us with an example.

Joel was a fairly new member to a well-established group. Part of the tradition established by group members was to have dinner together after group. The members found that it was a good opportunity to strengthen the bond between them and to develop a deeper sense of community. Going out together grew to be much more than a convenient way of eating. It was an emotionally charged ritual with a variety of levels of significance. The richness of this activity was largely unexplored until Joel challenged the whole notion.

Martha started group one week by saying to Joel, *"I'm disappointed you didn't come to dinner after group last week and hope you can come tonight."* Joel answered quite bluntly *"I don't want to go and I'm not going to."* The members were quick to express their hurt and anger. They perceived it as a personal rejection. Joel went on to say that he believed the group was trying to "brainwash" him. Going out to dinner was yet another example of his fellow ACOAs trying to control his life. He did not believe he should be held accountable to anyone. He believed that he was fundamentally on his own and that life was supposed to be that way. He also viewed the idea of processing major decisions in group as *"having you tell me what to do."* He resisted making regular phone calls to group members because he viewed it as *"people checking up on me."* Socializing with members at parties was avoided because *"I have better things to do."*

Another aspect to consider is that Joel could not believe that people in group cared for him. He judged himself harshly. To rely on others was a sign of weakness and failure. *"I should be able to do this by myself."* He had no conception that people could know him in depth and still want to be with him. Joel was actually pushing people away before they had a chance to reject him first. Paradoxically, his hostile and harsh behavior was an attempt to provoke the other members into rejecting him and thus confirming his own view of himself. It would be a combination of *"See they really were not different from my parents"* and *"I really am as bad as I thought."*

Joel had many scars as a result of alcoholism. His alcoholic father was harshly critical and physically abusive to him. In his early adolescence when his father's drinking got totally out of control, Joel went to a priest to seek help. The priest turned out to have alcoholism and sexually abused him as well. Finally, Joel developed alcoholism himself and did all the things he swore he would never do. It's no wonder he had such a sense of self-loathing and a powerful mixture of yearning and rage toward people who were trying to help or reach out to him.

Going out to dinner provided the arena for a clash between very powerful forces. On one side was Joel with his self-loathing and resistance to opening himself to the other ACOAs. On the other side were the members who had their own desire/need to "make things right," not be rejected and maintain a rigid defensive structure based on doing what was expected of them. The areas of belonging, rejection, control, and self-worth are crucial to persons raised in alcoholic families. These areas were central to the issue and ensured that the conflict that arose was rich with fundamental issues for the group members.

Joel viewed going out to dinner as an effort by group members to control him. He was adamant that he would not be told what to do. *"I'm an adult and shouldn't have to need you to run my life."* In essence, Joel was in group to **learn** how to live rather than to **experience** a communal process. He wanted to gain knowledge so he could do better running his own life, rather than develop a manner of living that was open to and shared with others. He did not want others to get close. *"I don't have anything else to do, but I sure don't want to go to dinner."*

At first the members almost begged Joel to give them a chance. Dan said, *"I take your not going as a reflection on me."*

Nellie said, *"I really want you to like me."* Others pointed out that he owed it to himself to give it a chance. Martha wondered if she were wrong to have expressed her disappointment to begin with. It played into her long-standing fear that if she expressed disappointment or made her needs known to somebody she cared for, then the person would either ignore her or leave. The initial theme was, *"If somebody doesn't want to join with me, then something must be wrong with me."* As a result, members wondered if they were being too rigid. Maybe they were asking too much of Joel. However, the more people talked, their self-doubt was replaced with anger toward Joel.

Sue said, *"It doesn't make sense that you could come to group and then not go out to dinner."* Others took it as a sign that Joel wasn't serious about recovery, *"AA says if you want to recover, you will go to any length. We're telling you this is necessary."* The anger, in turn, led to a third level of emotion; a sense of empathetic desperation. They could see Joel slipping away, not so much from them, but from his best chance at recovery.

Members were so emphatic about the need for Joel to go to dinner, make phone calls, and involve the members in his life because they truly believed that these activities rescued them from lives of despair. Each one had stood at the turning point that Joel had reached. Members could offer no rational reason why they went to dinner when they were terrified of the other people; why they asked the opinion of others even though they were certain of their plans; or why they were able to ask for help despite vowing to be self-sufficient. The consensus was that all an ACOA could do was to show up, be open, and leave the rest to a Higher Power. That is why they pushed for Joel to just show up. It was one aspect of his recovery that he could do something about, and they saw it slipping away.

Joel's situation allowed members to personalize the topic of belonging and reaching out. Alcoholism had robbed their parents of the ability to provide them with unconditional nurturance. Their parents were unable to create an atmosphere of stability and security in which children can flourish as individuals, yet still have the family as a foundation for support. It was easier for the group members to focus on Joel than it was for them to explore how they had been affected in similar ways.

Frank talked about being desperate to resolve conflict in his family. He believed the best he could hope for in his family was the

absence of explosive conflict. He would serve as the family medi-
ator, going back and forth between various members trying to
settle actual, or prevent potential, conflicts. His role in a family or
community was to prevent problems from exploding. It was hard
for him to realize that one can hope to get things from a family,
that a family can actually provide its members with well-being. He
tried to deny his own needs for a greater good.

Pete shared how he sometimes viewed himself as a nonentity.
Regarding group he said, *"One of the reasons I come every week
is because I'm afraid no one will notice if I'm not here."* Pete used
being invisible as his main method of getting by. Being invisible
was useful to him in surviving his childhood, but the deep loneliness it created had made reaching out very difficult. Martha
revealed how desperate she was to get the attention of her alcoholic father. Her main image of him was sitting at the kitchen table
drinking beer, smoking cigarettes, and staring off into space. She
remembered trying all sorts of things to get through to him. She
would show him things she made, ask him questions about his job,
and do favors for him, but still she could not break through to him.
She found it easy to get mad at Joel for not letting her into her life,
but it still was scary for her to think about being mad at her own
father for the same reasons.

Joanne confessed that she had removed herself from the
whole situation regarding Joel. She had been feeling a sense of
desolation and just "turned off" until it all blew away. She recalled
losing herself in reading as a child. *"I would just hide behind a
book while chaos swirled around me."* She viewed taking a stand
or involving herself in the process as requiring the investment of
too much energy in an unsolvable situation.

The reason there was so much conflict and depth of feeling
was that going out to dinner was not the main issue. It was only a
vehicle for the ACOAs to reenact and explore some major themes
and components of their syndrome. It brought to the surface the
conflict between yearning to reach out and belong to a family or
community (i.e., group) as opposed to the desire to be self-sufficient and maintain control while resisting the threatening over-
tures of others who claimed to care, but would ultimately be
rejecting (Joel).

Joel had an intuitive sense that if he went to dinner he would
be taking the initial steps toward opening himself to others and
relinquishing his self-sufficiency. The other group members had

the sense that exploring their zeal in trying to get Joel to belong might provide them with the key to freeing themselves from ongoing efforts to get from people what they are incapable of giving. This situation with Joel also gave rise to more general questions. *"By insisting members become deeply involved in the life of the group, do we drive them away? What demands, if any, can we place on each other? By not pushing someone, do we create a conspiracy of silence? How do we deal with someone who insists on remaining isolated? What is the the nature of our obligation to each other?"* The unifying force behind all of these questions was the opportunity the ACOAs had to explore, examine, and define their relationships with each other. This was a radical departure from the sense of imposition and silent acquiescence that alcoholism gave rise to. In addressing these tough issues, ACOAs were affirming their own sense of self-worth and the value they place on the worth of others.

Expressing silly thoughts about friends buying a house and being disappointed over someone's not going out to dinner at first glance seem insignificant. These things, which many ACOAs viewed as minor and not important enough to bring up, provided the opportunity for major breakthroughs for a number of people. Having the courage and grace to be committed enough to each other to make mistakes or be embarrassed provided ACOAs with freedom. This freedom provided a deeper sense of self and richer relationship with each other. The ACOA therapy group gave its members the chance to explore and expand, rather than protect and defend relationships. Nellie and Joel were at different places on the same journey. Their relationships with the other members reflected the same issues, but from a different perspective. All were faced with the task of attempting to love themselves and accept and believe in the caring of others. If Laura and Nellie seemed more hopeful than did Joel, it was only because their scars and wounds were not as deep. Each of them had something to offer each other and the rest of the group. They reflected hope for what life could be, reminded one another of how destructive alcoholism is and how fortunate each one was to have a chance to be healed.

SUMMARY POINTS

I. TRUE COLLABORATION IS INDICATIVE OF AN ACOA'S RE-
COVERY. Joining together to initiate, plan, and complete a
project represents a high level of health for an ACOA. It
shows a sense of trust in another person and a belief that the
individual is no longer alone. How Laura and Nellie bought
their house is much more important than its actual purchase.

2. SELF-CENSORSHIP, INSTEAD OF PROTECTING ACOAS' RE-
LATIONSHIPS, CAUSES BARRIERS. The fear that being honest
with Laura and Nellie would threaten their relationships
caused group members to pull back. This pulling back had
the opposite effect of protecting the relationship. Not only
did it put barriers between them but it also caused the other
members to doubt their own perceptions and motives.

3. SOCIALIZING CAN BE THE BEST THING FOR ACOA GROUP
MEMBERS AND IT ALSO CAN BE THE WORST. There is much
disagreement with the notion of group members' interacting
outside of group. It can create coehesiveness and a sense of
community and it can also foster cliques and exclusion. It is
best done in the context of twelve-step group participation
and with the mandate that what happens outside of group be
brought inside for discussion. The risks of socializing outside of group are outweighed by the benefits gained by a
population whose loss of a family is the hallmark of their
syndrome.

6

More Than Meets the Eye

Dan wanted to thank everyone. The members of his ACOA group had given him a lot of help during the previous week. His wife, Jerri, had gone to Florida for a week with their two best friends. Dan had said he was nervous because he had never been alone with the kids for so long. He knew he needed help. Throughout the week group members had called him, stopped by to visit, and invited him to their homes for dinner. Though he had been apprehensive about the week, as Jerri's vacation went on he discovered a sense of belonging he had not anticipated.

It would have been easy enough to stop right there. Certainly Dan didn't think there was anything left to discuss. The group, with its instinctive preference for problem solving, was congratulating itself for helping him. Dan was also feeling pretty good because he had allowed them to help him. Although it is true that Dan's reaching out for logistical support was an important milestone, it was only 20 percent of what needed to be explored. Nobody had mentioned his wife.

"How do you feel about Jerri's going to Florida without you?" This question set off alarms inside Dan. Immediately he became tense and wary. He gave a programmed answer, *"I'm glad she got the opportunity to go."* But by his posture and tone of voice, it was easy to tell he felt threatened and was becoming closed. When he was asked, *"What's it like talking to her on the phone?"* Dan was able to admit that their conversations were a bit awkward. He described the hard time he was having listening to her talk about the fun she was having. He felt bad because he thought he should be happy for her. He was also able to acknowledge he felt a bit angry at her for not calling more frequently.

That gave the group more to work with. This self-described "mild irritation" provided the key to further exploration and awareness. It was important to note that initially Dan did not regard the mild irritation as worthy of mention. The tiny inklings of emotion that ACOAs casually dismiss often indicate the presence of major, yet repressed, emotional turmoil. When asked, *"How do you feel toward her between phone calls?"* he was able to identify fear, which he believed was based on self-doubt. He wondered if she was having too much fun. He was afraid that her good time would highlight his own inadequacies. As much as he tried, he couldn't help but imagine her meeting another man and having an affair. As he talked, it became clear that being alone with the kids was only the presenting problem. The real issue was Dan's relationship with his wife.

The group was starting to catch on. It began to dawn on everyone that something was unusual. Most married people do not go on vacation with another couple and leave their spouses behind. This unleashed a great deal of emotion. The group reacted by getting mad at Jerri for Dan. *"You should have put your foot down."* *"I wouldn't have allowed her to go."* What triggered this reaction? It soon became apparent that the universal fear ACOAs have of being left out and not belonging had been tapped. At first Dan retreated and allowed the group to do the work for him. After listening to his peers react so strongly, he was able to grudgingly admit that he was "a little bit annoyed" that she went to Florida without him. However, he quickly countered with *"How can I be so selfish as to deny her this opportunity?"*

This denial of anger and disappointment combined with an exaggerated concern and care for Jerri have roots in the alcoholic family. It is not unusual for an ACOA to say *"I'm not mad at my parents anymore, how could I be mad at people who have a disease. I'm not disappointed because I know they did the best they could. I learned early not to expect anything from my parents."* The idea of becoming aware of the hurt caused by being rejected, abandoned, or simply ignored by an alcoholic parent is terrifying. It is terrifying not only in and of itself but also because it leads to something even more frightening; an intense feeling of anger that borders on rage. Not only does the ACOA feel this anger, but it produces guilt as well. It is unacceptable to feel this way toward parents you are supposed to love.

This pattern of repressed anger being transferred into a concern for others based on self-denial will be reenacted by the ACOA in most, if not all, intimate relationships. An other-focused structure is developed. Doing for others is intended to bring the ACOA closer to other people. Just the opposite occurs. Since the ACOA defines himself as a "helper," there are few opportunities for others to reach out to him. People view him as being one-dimensional. He in turn begins to feel twinges of resentment toward others because he feels unappreciated. This resentment turns into an attitude of superiority. The underlying assumption is *"I have no needs."* **At the same time he is helping people he is actually looking down on them.** It is difficult to penetrate the facade and get to this hostility.

As the discussion continued it became clear that the group wanted somebody to be wrong. They wanted a villain. The group was asked to consider that both Dan and Jerri had goodwill. Finding a villain was not necessary. Perhaps understanding would be more valuable than blame. They needed to go back to the beginning and see how the decision that Jerri go to Florida was made. That would reveal more about Dan's marriage and their own relationships than undergoing the process of attempting to assess guilt and assign blame. Assessing guilt and assigning blame are restrictive. They narrow the field of vision to two stark choices: right or wrong. Making a decision to explore for the purpose of understanding allows a richness to develop. As a result, awareness both of self and others can occur.

As the discussion continued, everyone in the group thought it would be valuable to see how Dan and Jerri made their decision. It had seemed so simple. Their friends were going to Florida, they knew Jerri was between jobs, and so they invited her to go with them. Since neither Dan nor Jerri had ever been to Florida, their first thought was that it would be a good opportunity for Jerri. In fact, Dan actually encouraged her to go. **It had never occurred to Dan to say he wanted to go as well.** He did not have any idea that he too would have liked to have gone on the trip. When questioned in group he said he never even considered the possibility of his going with them. To him it was simple. He was working and Jerri wasn't.

The truth was more complicated. The reason he denied any desire to be included in their trip was because **he wasn't invited.** This incident tapped into one of Dan's main fears: **the fear of being excluded and, as a result, shown to be inferior.** The last thing in the world he wanted was an overt rejection. He didn't ask to go along because he was terrified of being told no. He would adjust to the situation rather than take any direct action that might make it worse. Not making a direct request meant he would not have to face the possibility of direct rejection. The best way to avoid making a direct request, and maintain some level of freedom from anxiety, is to repress any desire to be included.

It is important to note that this repression was not a conscious act. Dan had little, if any, inkling of what was happening inside of him. As we noted before, the most he was aware of feeling was a mild annoyance and a vague fear. It was only with the help of his fellow ACOAs that he was able to have his thoughts and feelings become more available and less censored. The reason group was able to stay with him during this process was because the fear of being rejected or left out was shared by every ACOA in the room. As Dan talked, group members began to relate their own terror of directly asking for something. A simple request would be turned into a judgment on their very essence. In order to avoid this, some members had developed a "first-strike" defense. They would reject others before they themselves were rejected. **The preference was to be alone by choice, rather than be alone as a result of a perceived rejection.**

Looking back, Dan saw that he had to work harder to supress his anger. As the date of Jerri's departure drew closer, he censored any thoughts he might have had regarding his own needs or expectations of Jerri. The rationalization he provided for this supression was: *"What good would it do to get mad? She'd probably go anyway."* Anger was not the primary emotion. Although it was present, the main value of his anger was to indicate the presence of deeper and more pressing emotions. The anger both covered up and pointed to Dan's sense of loss, loneliness, and feeling left out.

As Dan talked, two things became clear. First was that he really did want to go with Jerri. It also became clear that he wanted to go with Jerri because he loved her. He was able to acknowledge that he had a romantic notion (which he was hesitant to admit) that it would be nice if they saw Florida for the first time together. Dan had covered these tender and touching thoughts and feelings by presenting technical objections to Jerri's going alone. (e.g., finances, job search, etc.) It was hard for him to allow himself to just feel sad that they wouldn't be together. *"I need you and I want to be with you"* got transformed into *"I'm nervous about your going because I don't know how to cook."*

Alcoholic families do not lend themselves to an open process of compromise and negotiation. ACOAs have few, if any, role models of family members working together to attempt to identify and accommodate various personal needs. Arbitrary edicts, manipulation, and resentful silence are the tools of decision making in an alcoholic family. With that legacy, it is no wonder that Dan was unable to identify his needs, much less express them. That is why he was not able to engage Jerri in a joint search for alternatives. Everything had to be cut and dried. The only thing to be considered was the original proposal with no thought of modification or deviation. An ironic point is that Jerri had actually wanted Dan to go with her, but she was just as trapped by these emotional constraints as he was.

With these themes exposed, Dan and the group were ready to look for alternatives. Dan had an insight that the whole situation would have been different if he had not waited to discuss it until Jerri had already left. This point is critical. **Dan waited so long and confined his talking to just logistical matters, because he had an instinctive fear of uncovering too much.** Feeling left out, jealous, helpless, and suspicious of Jerri would be painful to look at. It was important to keep it safe. That is why his interactions with group members were limited to asking for help with the kids and getting advice on how to get through the week.

As the discussion further continued, Dan saw there were many alternatives. He could have gotten time off from work himself. The kids could have gone to a baby-sitter or even have gone with them. He and Jerri could have turned it into a family trip and met the other couple in Florida. If he couldn't get a week off, he could have flown down on the weekend. It all boiled down to the fact that if he had processed it with Jerri and group from the start, there would have been a good chance he would have been in Florida also.

SUMMARY POINTS

1. ACOAS USUALLY HAVE MORE ALTERNATIVES THAN THEY REALIZE. In this case everyone in group was startled at the

number of alternatives. They were also stunned when they realized that when left to their own devices, they would not have thought of them either. The building of relationships and the give and take in an ACOA group actually give the members the opportunity to explore alternatives and make healthy decisions. Consultation and exploration become a way of life.

2. ACOAS NEED MORE THAN JUST BEING TAUGHT NEW DECI-SION-MAKING SKILLS. It must be made clear that the therapeutic work of exploring emotions, becoming aware of defenses, and examining the various themes of Dan's inter-actions set the stage for the development of alternatives. His previous decision-making process was based on long standing issues that needed to be addressed. They did not exist in a vacuum. They reflected emotional defenses that needed to be explored. **ACOAs cannot be taught out of their syndrome.** That is why the best approaches involve a combination of psychodynamic exploration as well as the development of alternative methods of interacting. These are combined and held together by a sense of community and spirituality based on the twelve-step programs.

3. REACHING OUT IS ESSENTIAL TO AN ACOA'S RECOVERY. This example showed the value of the ACOA group as a community. The social network and logistical help provided by ACOA group members develop a foundation of caring and acceptance. Dan reached out for help in managing his household during Jerri's trip. The group responded and opened their homes to him and shared his life with him during that week. That gave him the security necessary to explore in group the depth of his feelings. The combination of reaching out and acceptance created an atmosphere that allowed everyone to go beyond problem solving and toward self-revelation. It created a bond and sense of belonging. Their common bond enabled them then to explore with a new vision more productive ways of relating. By not settling for mere problem solving, a deeper community was formed and self-awareness increased.

4. ACOAS USUALLY HAVE A RIGID VIEW OF PROPER AND IMPROPER THOUGHTS. This prevents them from identifying and exploring their own feelings. Since they are preoccupied with protecting a relationship from what they perceive as very threatening conflicts, when they do get an inkling of their own needs they are often unable to be direct. Hints and innuendos are used much more often than a straightforward approach. As a result, their needs often go unmet. In this case, Dan's fear of expressing his own need actually led him to encourage Jerri to go on her trip; at the same time, he was feeling angry and resentful.

7

Dare I Ask for More?

Evan had declared his homosexuality, but had never talked about it fully. He gave the appearance that he was at peace with his sexuality and, not surprisingly, no one in group ever questioned him. Periodically he attempted to find out if any of the other ACOAs had problems with his sexuality. In fact, when he first came into group he was quite aggressive in setting people straight if they had any misconceptions or deviated from the "party line."

As time went on, Evan became one of the pillars of the group. Members looked to him for support and could always count on his being available. As his relationship with group members blossomed, his sexuality remained vaguely off-limits with no one venturing to include it as a topic of discussion. In one sense it became like a piece of landscape that was seen yet unseen.

Both Evan and the other ACOAs were utilizing two common defenses. Evan's defense was to give an overly aggressive response to any hint of inquiry into the topic of his homosexuality. The "correctness" of its content disguised the aggressiveness of his response. *"This is the way it is and this is the way it should be. So you had better examine your bias and watch your step."* Very few people would brave that mine field.

The group's defenses were to subscribe to a "correct" way of thinking and consider the subject closed. Because their thoughts were correct, they were able to maintain a false sense that the issue had been resolved. It also created strong peer pressure against one of them returning to the topic. Not only would the individual have to wade through Evan's mine field, but he would have to say everyone else was wrong when each closed the issue.

One day Evan had a major breakthrough in group. He started

to share the anguish he had experienced as a result of his sexuality. He told of being trapped in his marriage and trying to fake being heterosexual. He was able to share the shame and fear he felt in trying to lead two lives. For the first time he revealed how lost he was during his days of cruising and having anonymous sex. It was a true catharsis that had been a long time coming. For the first time in group Evan revealed the depth of who he was and unburdened the guilt and pain he had been carrying for so long. During this process he began to realize that by sharing all about his sexuality he became a whole person. Previously he had been viewing himself primarily through his sexual orientation. Through the process of revelation and trust he began to view his homosexuality as a part of himself, rather than his entire self.

Lacking a sense of self, ACOAs tend to define themselves by their actions. This does not only apply to the area of sexuality. Self-definition is often based on external accomplishments or situations (e.g., *"I must be acceptable because I'm married." "If I don't get a 4.0 GPA, I'll just die." "My boss really needs me because I'm so organized."*). The main problem is that external accomplishments cannot fill the void created by a lack of self-worth and self-acceptance. External rewards are not enough to fill internal voids. The quest to focus on and/or acquire attributes is essentially conducted under false pretenses. These externals only serve as a substitute for what they are actually seeking: self-love and a sense of belonging.

The group was awestruck by Evan's catharsis and by his vulnerability. Many told him how moved they were and grateful that he chose to share his feelings with them. While thanking him, they stated how close they felt to him. The group then moved on to the next topic.

A subtle change happened in Evan after that night. At first not much thought was given to it, but it proved to be significant. He didn't follow up on his breakthrough in the ensuing weeks. This is not to say that he stopped participating. His activity in group became more focused on helping others. There was a slight distance or a casual formality in his interactions. His insights and comments remained accurate and penetrating, but they also began to develop a harsh edge. He began to become impatient with members who couldn't get the message and straighten up right away. There was a tinge of anger in his attitude.

During the same time he began to talk about "graduating" from group. He wanted to know what, if anything, he had to do before he could leave. A time line was desired so he could plan accordingly. It is always important to note the recent group activity of a person who is discussing leaving group. The history and context are of more value than the initially stated reasons. The change in the pattern of Evan's behavior in group, combined with his desire to leave, indicated that there was an unresolved issue that needed to be brought to the surface. In most people's eyes Evan was progressing in good form. He had just had a moving experience that had pushed him to a new level. Yet, instead of the expected response, he was talking about leaving. Why now? was the question that had to be answered. It was necessary to search to see the source of his desire to leave.

Talking in individual therapy, Evan discovered that these thoughts of leaving coincided with his talking about his sexuality. He reported that he had simply pushed the incident from his mind and moved on. He didn't think it was a big deal. **What happened in that group, however, was a huge deal!** It was a major breakthrough, but for Evan something was missing. Upon reflection he realized that his feelings were hurt. Even though the group's response was appropriate, it wasn't what he needed.

In Evan's eyes an **appropriate** response wasn't enough. His anger and hurt over receiving only an appropriate response were hidden from his consciousness yet they were readily apparent in his behavior in subsequent groups. His actions toward others became **very appropriate**: No more and no less. This explained the sense of distance and anger that people intuited from Evan's actions in group. He was giving back to them the same reserved response he believed they had given to him.

Evan wanted to be fussed over. He wanted group members to aggressively reach out and make a big deal about how they loved and cared for him. Just stating their affection for him wasn't enough. He wanted to be praised and affirmed for a long time. He later said he felt an almost physical need to have people jump up and down cheering for him and crush him in hugs. He wanted to know that they really knew the enormity of what he did. It was a primal yearning that needed to be filled. He wanted to be actively drawn out and made whole.

Evan also felt silly and embarrassed over these desires. *"I shouldn't feel this way. Everyone said they were moved by what I discussed. Why should I need special attention?"* He couldn't figure out why an adult would need such things. *"I don't know why I'm feeling this way."*

Coming from an alcoholic family is the perfect explanation of why he felt that way. Alcoholism had robbed his parents of the ability to express unconditional love, nurturing, and acceptance. As a result, Evan had to deny the yearning he had to be loved, nurtured, and accepted unconditionally. He also had to deny the pain, anger, and emptiness he felt as a result of not having been given what he believed he needed. He had never allowed himself the opportunity for unreserved joining with others. He wanted to be internally self-sufficient. A facade of competence developed that gave no hint of the depth of his yearnings. He had made numerous attempts at frantic coupling with various types of people, but there was always a part that remained impenetrable and reserved. Behind that barricade was a thought that kept saying, "Why bother, it won't work."

This unrestrained letting go that Evan was so afraid of was the very thing he wanted group members to give to him. By sharing so deeply, he allowed himself to dare to hope that others would celebrate who he was. The problem was that Evan could not identify, and then allow to dissolve, that internal reserve which barricaded his emotions and kept part of himself hidden. **He had not given group any hint that he needed more from them or that he felt incomplete.**

In preparing to return to group, Evan had to explore many things. He had to decide if all this was worth the pain and effort. He had to figure out if he really wanted to explore and examine the need to be cared for. He was afraid that if he allowed this yearning for love to surface, he might lose control and be engulfed by pain. Even worse, if he asked for it he might be refused. Perhaps it would be easier to keep the facade intact. His intellect believed that he would not be refused, yet he was still afraid. This doubt came from a sense that he was not worthy of that caring. This lack of self-worth came not from anything he had **done**. Instead it came from his own sense of who he was.

A leap of faith was required. Going to group and returning to this topic was a graced act that required enormous courage. It was easier to share his cruising and sexual escapades than to share his yearning to be embraced by the group members. **How could he tell them that their reasonable response wasn't enough for him?** How could he tell them that he needed much more? His relationship with group kindled a spark that he thought had died long ago. Not only did he believe he had given up hope of finding the love his parents were unable to give him, but he also believed he didn't need it. Group changed that.

The group had an equally difficult task. Their first area of difficulty was his homosexuality. The second was their reaction to someone's being so out-loud about needing them greatly.

In the beginning no one mentioned anything about homosexuality, because they were afraid of Evan's aggressive response. After his catharsis, no one would admit to any difficulties regarding homosexuality, because they felt guilty about having them. They especially didn't want to hurt Evan after being so moved by him. As a result, most gave him "correct" responses, if they said anything at all. *"I love you as a person." "Your sexuality doesn't mean anything to me." "I don't think of you as gay."* In truth his sexuality was on everyone's mind. (Some were more successful than others in repressing it.) There is a mistaken notion that love and acceptance cannot coexist with instinctive negative or fearful reactions. The belief is that doubts and problems can't be discussed because it might drive the person away. Because they cared for Evan deeply, they tended to automatically say they had no problem with his homosexuality and squelch any negative feelings.

Homosexuality is not a neutral topic for ACOAs. Just being a member of this society makes it a loaded issue. ACOAs have added baggage. Many have gender identity issues. They may have been sexually abused by the same-sex parent while the parent was intoxicated, and those who drank may have had homosexual experimentations while they were under the influence of alcohol. These experiences haven't been resolved and they often skew any interactions regarding sexuality. A deepening relationship with Evan does not preclude honest exploration of thoughts, feelings, and attitudes among group members. The reverse is actually true. Being in a relationship and seeing that his humanity transcends his sexuality make it possible for group members to share about their own sexuality.

The group members also had to face the issues that arose

from someone's having a great need for them. Right away it brings up reactions that had their formation in childhood. In alcoholic families, parents (both alcoholic and nonalcoholic) place inappropriate expectations and needs on their children. Children are not developmentally ready to even hear, let alone address, most of these demands. They range from having to take physical care of a parent incapacitated by drunkenness to providing emotional care by serving as the nonalcoholic parent's main confidant and source of support. To be needed means to be smothered with unreasonable and never ending demands. Most importantly these are demands that can never be met, thus creating a sense of guilt and inadequacy. Although some ACOAs unconsciously attempt to recreate these type of relationships, most react with fear when a need such as Evan's is stated in such an open and heartfelt manner.

Group provided a forum for overcoming this reluctance. Being in community gave the members the chance to honestly explore their thoughts and feelings.

They did not have to give Evan a correct response. Freed by the depth of their commitment to Evan, they were able to be honest. They saw that his desire made them both glad and scared, glad that Evan thought enough of them to desire to join with them, and scared that his demands would be too much and they would either fail him or be smothered. They also discovered that the more honest and open they were while they were exploring this, the more the fear diminished.

These ACOAs were able to distinguish between the reactions based on the past and the reality of the present situation. Before, if too much was asked of them, they felt trapped and could think of no alternatives. Now they had a process that gave them the ability to share their thoughts and make healthy judgments. Both the request and the decision-making process were out in the open.

In the end, the group could not resist Evan's honest vulnerability. His considered leap of faith caused their hesitancy to dissolve. It was an example of the spirituality of the recovery process. There was more to it than the sum of its parts. Evan's faith and the group's acceptance cannot be adequately explained in clinical terms. Universal yearnings were played out and they awakened in the other members a similar need they too had tried to ignore or downplay. The whole process can best be summed up by paraphrasing a line from the poem **The Hound of Heaven** "Fear wist not to evade, as love wist to pursue."[1]

SUMMARY POINTS

1. ANY ASPECT OF SEXUALITY IS AN EMOTIONALLY CHARGED TOPIC IN AN ACOA GROUP. Rhetoric and clichés often replace inquiry and revelation when sex and sexuality are discussed.

2. THERE IS A TENDENCY TO GIVE CORRECT, GUARDED RESPONSES TO THE PERSON TALKING. As a result, the members become an audience watching and helping a particular individual. The goal in group should be to create an environment in which one person's sharing can create a trigger that allows others, not only to help that individual but to reveal themselves as well.

3. THE INABILITY OF ALCOHOLIC PARENTS TO GIVE UNCONDITIONAL LOVE AND AFFIRMATION CREATES A YEARNING IN ACOAS THAT IS OFTEN OUT OF CONSCIOUS AWARENESS, YET COLORS ALL OF THEIR SIGNIFICANT RELATIONSHIPS. ACOAs do not give up the yearning for parental love as they grow older. Instead this yearning gets repressed and transformed into other pursuits. Recovery provides them a forum to identify and acknowledge these repressed or transformed needs. In community with others they can trace how these yearnings have formed recurrent themes throughout their lives. As a result, they can then develop healthy, realistic alternatives to satisfy the need to be cared for.

4. ACOAS HAVE A FEAR OF ASKING FOR TOO MUCH. Being direct is often seen as threatening what already exists. To ask for more puts in jeopardy what is already there. There is a sense that any caring or acceptance is more than they ex-

---

[1] Francis Thompson, "The Hound of Heaven," *A Little Treasury of Modern Poetry,* ed, Oscar Williams (1893), p. 599.

pected, so it's best not to push their luck too far. Unfortunately, relying on having your needs met by guesswork causes resentment when the guesses inevitably miss the mark. The resulting anger and withdrawal cause the very distance that the defenses were employed to avoid.

8

I Dare You to Like Me

Lois had never really dated. She had focused most of her energy on developing a self-sufficient life. She had been fairly successful in obtaining a nice job and creating a secure, though compartmentalized, life. Although she was a very competent person, she was filled with self-doubt. Her mind was frequently occupied with attempting to keep the various parts of her life functional and running smoothly. She would plan, think, worry, and analyze. It was as if she believed that her life would begin to fall apart if she wasn't vigilant. Her interactions with people, though generally correct and polite, were designed to maintain a safe distance. People were too unpredictable. After all they would only let her down if she began to depend on them and let them get too close.

Lois was very good at her job. Unfortunately she did not enjoy her work and her colleagues did not enjoy working with her. She was demanding of herself and intolerant of others. She would project onto others the inadequacies she felt about herself. Her colleagues believed she had few, if any, endearing traits. She was so captured by her fear that she was stunned to see that it had turned into arrogance. The painful twist was that instead of making her more secure, her actions and defenses were only increasing her alienation.

Lois worked very hard. She would work through lunch and not take breaks. It was hard for her to work as part of a team. A serious grim expression was very effective in placing her outside of the workplace mainstream. She would not tolerate any joking, silliness, or teasing. She would be quick to put into place anyone who did not treat her with the dignity and seriousness she deserved.

It would surprise her to think that people pictured her as being arrogant and aloof. She saw herself as frightened and working really hard to keep up at work. She covered up her desire to be "part of the gang" by looking down her nose at them. She employed her first-strike defense because she truly believed she had to preempt being taken advantage of or fired. On the surface she appeared cool, calm, and collected, while on the inside she was running scared. She couldn't understand why no one could see how vulnerable she was even though she came across as less vulnerable than Margaret Thatcher.

Lois had no idea how to lighten up. Because competence shielded her lack of self-worth, she could not let her guard down. Every action and encounter was approached with great gravity because each one had, in her eyes, the potential to unmask her as a fraud. Her self-definition depended upon her continuing successful performances. It was essential that she set the stage and control all the variables. Her life was essentially reactive and defensive. Nothing could be left to chance. Her energy was expended battling to keep her head above water and remain one step ahead of the perceived inevitable catastrophe. She had a vague premonition that she could not keep up the pace for much longer.

On a social level, Lois rigidly adhered to the proprieties. She could always be counted on to recognize birthdays, send thank you notes, call before coming over, entertain properly, and know what each occasion called for. **Life's major points were duly noted but never shared.** This extreme approach to relating also required her to keep score. Keeping score caused major problems in two directions. First, it fed a sense of superiority. She was doing the correct things while nobody else was. It set her apart from the hoi polloi. She was the one who really cared. Second, it served as a justification for her self-sufficiency. She had been wronged. *"I do all these things for people and no one does anything for me." "I really have tried, but I'm still on my own."* Her rigidity in this area was not as subtle as she would have liked to have believed. Lois did not realize how her friends panicked at the thought of forgetting her birthday. They would have preferred the ordeal of root canal without anesthesia to visiting her unannounced.

One of the main themes in her life was that happiness would be found elsewhere. She was always looking for an exotic, faraway place where she would find happiness. Talking about moving to

Turkey or the Fiji Islands was when Lois was the most animated. Clinging to this notion of getting away allowed her to not put down roots. There was no need for commitment. Since wherever she was living was only temporary, there was no reason to be vulnerable. She claimed to have no emotional expectations of others. She knew she might be moving soon. Lois turned the cliché "Nothing ventured, nothing gained" into "Nothing ventured, nothing lost."

Alcoholism had scattered Lois's family. The main goal of each of her brothers and sisters was to get as far away as possible. The purpose of the family diaspora was to seek happiness. No one knew where to look, but everyone knew that it could not be found at home. The family members would drift from place to place and job to job with no internal compass or external healthy point of reference. Succeeding in changing only their surroundings, internally each began to replicate the same paths taken by their alcoholic parents.

Lois eventually joined an ACOA group. Typically, she at first viewed it as only a way station on her quest for something else. *"It would be good for me to be here while I figure out where I want to go and what I want to do."* Her coming to group was similar to a car's going to be serviced. She wanted to fix and improve what already existed and then move on. She wanted to learn how to get away quicker and more comfortably. As the process began to work, Lois, almost without knowing it, began to put down roots.

The first step was that she accepted the invitation to enter the lives of her fellow group members. She heard people sharing their hopes and fears. She saw people working through problems openly while relying on others. They included her and actively sought her input. Enjoying that, she then felt secure enough to invite them into hers. Her "social correctness" actually became a group legend. She would call people on a regular basis and began to spend a lot of time with them. Her first fight with another group member provided her first highlight in group. She was very excited, though she recognized it after the fact. She had never done that before. The two of them actually got angry and quarreled! It made for an unpleasant couple of days, but the conflict got resolved openly and directly.

It was the first time Lois had a healthy fight. Usually she would say something sarcastic and then retreat to lick her wounds while developing a sense of moral superiority. Before too long she would be viewing herself as Mother Theresa while her friend would be the scum of the earth. The relationship would be seriously damaged and not be back on track for months, if at all. That's why she would avoid fights at all costs. Too much was at stake. Arguments meant an all-out fight to the finish. To protect herself from herself and avoid unleashing this onslaught, Lois would just look down on the person and return when the other person would come to her senses. When they did get back together nothing was said.

This fight was different. Lois was open about her thoughts and feelings; she waited until her anger had died down and processed what happened with the other person. It reflected a commitment not only to herself but to the other person. She cared enough to take a risk. The purpose of the fight was to join together with another person rather than destroy her.

This entering into community with other ACOAs paved the way for Lois's second step. She began to bring what she was receiving in group into work. She began to be viewed differently on the job. Being accepted by others in group gave her increased confidence which in turn allowed her to lower her guard at work. She became less adversarial and aloof. She began to take little steps that eased the tension. She decided she didn't have to work longer and harder than anybody else. She took her full lunch hour and tried not to sit alone in the cafeteria. Not acting like a snob was one of her main priorities. She started to take breaks and banter with her colleagues. She even went as far as to ask their advice on a number of projects, even though she really didn't think she needed it.

Lois was starting to view herself as valuable, not only as a person, but as an employee as well. She would actually believe her excellent job performance reviews. She no longer suspiciously viewed promotions as part of a grand scheme to expose her as an incompetent fraud. She saw that they really did mean that her employers wanted her to advance. They were not setting her up in order to fire her. Most importantly, she was now considering herself worthy of advancement.

The progress in both of these areas led to a stable period for Lois. This period of rest was not wasted. It was a period where she internalized and digested what had happened. She was consolidating her gains and enjoying the fellowship of her peers. After a time she realized it was time to face another major area: romance.

Lois joined a dating service. She had no real hope that it would be successful, but she viewed it as a base that had to be covered. Other than "to get dates" Lois had no notion of what to expect. The dating was categorized as yet another activity, the same as golfing or doing the laundry. However, it meant much more. Lois spent so much time focusing on the mechanics of dating that she was removed from any feeling. She could not take the time to explore the implications of this act and the path on which she was embarking.

Over the course of six months, Lois had numerous dates. All were similar in their stunning lack of success. Week after week she would announce one flop after another. Because people felt badly for her, no one pressed her to explore what was happening. They just cheered and encouraged her. Finally a group member took the plunge. He stated the obvious; something wasn't working, and he asked her to go over step by step what happened on the dates. Up until this point Lois would simply proclaim the flop of one date and the scheduling of another. There was no room for discussion. Lois discovered that it was easier to announce that a date didn't work out and just end the discussion. Failure was expected, so there was no need to beat a dead horse. It was quite different and scary to talk about what she did and how she felt on a date. Entering into those areas would reveal her huge insecurities about her ability to be romantically involved and her suitability as a partner.

Her feelings about dating were quite similar to those she used to have on the job. She would be scared and insecure before a date. To compensate she would put on her best and competent "I'm your equal. I can do for myself" act. She did not want to appear like a "helpless female." Lois more than succeeded in that. She came across as invulnerable with no interest in making the date work. *"He didn't even try to kiss me after I paid for the bill, got his coat, walked him to his car, and shook his hand."* She would bludgeon the guy with her self-sufficiency.

Lois would also never allow the full scope of her beauty to show. She was always careful to dress in an asexual manner, wearing the least revealing clothes possible for a first date. She wanted to make sure guys would be attracted to her for her brains and skills. *"I didn't want to give anybody the wrong impression."* She made great efforts to keep the date as casual as possible with no hint of romance. She sent very clear messages that the evening was about having dates and fulfilling social requirements, not setting the stage for romance. She was afraid even to entertain the hope of finding a partner. In her eyes it was better to have something not get started than to try and be hurt if it did not work out.

Lois was becoming discouraged. She was engaged in a self-fulfilling prophecy that proved her negative expectations. *"I knew nothing would happen, but I figured I'd give it a shot anyhow."* She was setting herself up to fail. As long as she kept on dating, she could claim she was doing the best that she could. As long as she kept on being unsuccessful, she would never have to look at her fear of being involved in a healthy romance. The pain of unsuccessful attempts at dating actually shielded her from facing the fear and pain she felt regarding her adequacy.

During this period she had a very brief sexual fling with an unhealthy "blast from the past." She said she wanted to prove to herself that she could have sex with someone. Talking about the fling in group was a turning point. She wasn't condemned. Everyone was understanding and most had done similar things. Lois figured if no one jumped on her for jumping on him, it was safe for her to talk about what she was ashamed of on a deeper level.

The words finally came. *"I don't know how to go on a date. I just don't know what to do."* Here was freedom. She didn't have to pretend any longer. She didn't have to hide the fact that she had no practical experience with dating. Most of her sexual experiences had been drunken encounters. These encounters left her feeling lost with no means of escape. At her age, Lois was ashamed to admit she couldn't do what she perceived any fifteen-year-old could do. (That's an inaccurate perception about fifteen-year-olds.) Lois said it was one of the most difficult admissions she had ever had to make. Now all of her cards were on the table. With the pressure off, Lois could share fully with group the entire process of her dating. There was no longer any need to hide, limit discussion, or present a facade of competence.

The third and eleventh steps of Alcoholics Anonymous are crucial. It is typical that when ACOAs resign from self-directed hard work and rely on vulnerability and openness, things often happen. Lois was no exception. Soon afterward she met a guy she really liked. Donald was everything she had looked for in a guy. Instead of being happy when she found out Donald really liked her, Lois got scared and began to have doubts. She wondered if he was too normal and too nice. *"I'm not used to something good."* Suddenly the stakes had been raised. **Lois was experiencing the terror of increased expectations.** This relationship actually had a chance of working. That had never happened to her before. She had had a lot of practice dealing with the feelings generated by not meeting the right guy. Now she was overwhelmed by combined fears of not wanting to like somebody too much along with being afraid she would do something to blow it.

Lois expressed concern because *"he likes me too much."* She said she didn't want to encourage him because *"I don't want to hurt him."* In fact the opposite was true. She was really talking about herself. *"I'm afraid because I like him so much. If I get serious I may get hurt."* In her mind there was an even bigger problem. What about our first fight? She was panic stricken. *"If I fight with him, he may see who I really am and it may destroy our relationship."*

Lois was also terrified to tell Donald about her alcoholic family, her own alcoholism, and her being in AA and therapy. This showed the depth of her lack of self-acceptance. She didn't know if it was necessary to share her "story" with him, even though her recovery was the most important thing in her life. She was starting a serious, romantic relationship with Donald, yet she wanted to keep 80 percent of her life secret. Lois thought it would be too much for him to handle. She was projecting her own sense of embarrassment and unworthiness onto him. *"If he really knew me he'd change his mind."* When she finally did tell him, his response was very positive. It turned out that the openness and vulnerability she had developed in her recovery were the very things that attracted him to her.

Her ACOA group provided Lois with a community she could use for support. It also served as a family with which she could share and process the roller coaster of early love. In her family of origin, secrecy was a means of security and protection.

Now she could not wait to bring the latest news to group. Lois would alternate between being giddy one week and fatalistic the next. Each week would bring a new discovery. Throughout it all her friends just encouraged her. The caring and support of the group and the excitement of a new growing romance turned Lois into a new woman. She was lively and more sure of herself. This in turn nourished her relationship with Donald and it began to blossom. This romance did not diminish or come at the expense of her relationship with group. They both built upon each other.

Love was in bloom, but there were also problems. The stage was set for the clashing of Lois's independent life-style with the demands of a deepening romance. Her instinct was to view phone calls and planning as restrictive and intrusive as opposed to being fun, exciting, and necessary. When Donald came to watch her practice golf she was torn between thinking he was keeping tabs on her and being excited to see him. They also seemed to have diametrically opposed styles of housekeeping. Prim and proper Lois claimed that Donald, the slob, kept empty pizza boxes in his kitchen for a year. "Oh, the joys of romance!" Group was able to laugh and enjoy her "initiation." They pointed out that *The Odd Couple,* by Neil Simon, wasn't a successful play, movie, and television show by mistake. Conflict over these things is all part of the give and take of living in our society. Most couples experience it. Lois's background as an ACOA might have made it more acute, but being in group also gave her the resources to manage and resolve it.

"So, do you think this guy might be the one you'll marry?" Lois's heart leapt to her throat. She was stunned and scared. Finally, the question had been directly raised. She had always told herself that marriage wasn't for her. It was too restrictive. She was too set in her ways to change. The routines of her life were too comfortable. Marriage would interfere with her plans. *"I didn't intend on bringing anyone with me to the Fiji Islands."* Her whole life had been based on finding happiness somewhere else at some other time. Now she was finding it here and now. She had never believed it would happen.

Everyone recognized that Lois's reaction to the thought of marriage was really a reaction to her alcoholic parents. The trauma of ongoing parental bitterness and anger had scarred her. **She saw marriage as a painful slide into darkness and despair that would slowly choke any flicker of warmth, caring, and spontaneity.** Each partner would withdraw into a private world, surrendering pieces of self in order to maintain an outward sense of calm. She promised herself at an early age that she would never live like that. Having the all-or-nothing, black-or-white approach of most ACOAs, Lois kept that promise by practically ruling out marriage. She had convinced herself that marriage wasn't for her. This covered her deep fear that her marriage would be doomed to failure.

The security and acceptance provided by group members gave Lois the foundation to look at the pain of her parents' marriage and her fears for her own. She saw how her reactions to her parents had restricted her life and made her deny her longings. She had secretly dreamed of marriage for a long time. In fact, she had been sizing up Donald from the start, but she couldn't admit it. She had even imagined what their kids would be like!, *"It's so silly,"* Lois said. She didn't know that everyone did it. In accepting the invitation to share without self-censorship, Lois was able to see the reasons she was restricting herself and benefit from the freedom that vision generated. It also cleared the debris from the past so she would not unconsciously sabotage this current relationship. She realized that she was different from her parents. Recovery gave her resources that alcoholism had denied her parents.

ACOAs' romantic relationships cannot be viewed in a vacuum. The themes in their current romances are also present in group, work, and other areas of their lives. Most of these themes can be traced back to the damage alcoholism wrecked on their parents and themselves. The increase in self-worth that ACOAs derive from being in a community with others allows them to recognize these things and begin to resolve them. They need not be trapped by their past. Recovery consists of both resolving the trauma of the past and developing resources to live in the present.

In one sense it didn't really matter if Lois and Donald got married. Marriage was not necessary to her identity nor was it something she had to run from. She didn't have to marry in order to find herself or be made whole. Instead, it was now possible for Lois to have a healthy marriage precisely because she had found herself and she had already been made whole. That was the gift of recovery.

SUMMARY POINTS

1. OFTEN THE DEFENSES ACOAS EMPLOY TO FORESTALL RE-JECTION CAUSE THE VERY REJECTION THEY ARE TRYING TO AVOID. ACOAs are so good at masking their fear and vulnerability that they often appear invulnerable and unapproachable. When others react to their masks of not needing anyone and do stay away, it fuels their fear and reinforces their defenses. This leaves ACOAs wondering why people don't approach them at the very time they are actively brushing them off.

2. CONSOLIDATION TIME IS VERY IMPORTANT TO THE RE-COVERY PROCESS OF ACOAS. They often grasp theoretical concepts without any internalization. Starting with feeling accepted by group, the themes of their problems are played out in one area after another. These themes are exposed and resolved in safe, less conflictual areas first and work their way toward areas of greater vulnerability and pain.

3. GROWING UP WITH ALCOHOLIC PARENTS GIVES ACOAS WARPED PERSPECTIVES ABOUT MARRIAGE. They generally react to the trauma and disintegration of their parents' marriage in two extremes. At one extreme, some idealize marriage and search for the perfect partner. They believe this partner will rescue them and together they will find heaven on earth. At the other extreme, ACOAs deny any desire to get married. Marriage is pessimistically viewed as not worth the pain. They say it is merely a social convention for which they have no use. Any yearning to be married is repressed under a variety of diversions and rationalizations.

9

Fragility Disguising Rage

Even though Lynn had been very pleasant, no one knew her. She had been in group for over two years but she had never really joined. Rarely did she initiate a discussion in group. Outside of group she resisted calling other members and avoided going to self-help meetings. During group she presented as scared, fragile, and confused. Very little was known or discussed about her day-to-day life. In the past she had disclosed vague memories of sexual abuse by her relatives and also revealed that she had gotten angry at her mother. Instead of these brief hints of revelation serving to increase her openness, they actually reinforced her defenses.

In general she was liked by the other members. She had put them off in such a pleasant manner, they didn't realize that she had done very little during the course of her time in group. Her particular defense of being pleasant while appearing fragile worked well. She appeared earnest and often said how she wished she would talk more. As a result the other members handled her with kid gloves. They treated the tiniest morsel of self-revelation as if it were a landmark breakthrough. It never occurred to them to ask her to do more or to give more of herself.

A group session devoted to reviewing her progress helped break the logjam. It was time to be direct with her. The time spent in group could be viewed as necessary to give her a period of adjustment and security. However, to let it continue without addressing what was happening would do both Lynn and the other members a disservice. There comes a time in every ACOA's recovery when she has to declare herself. She needs to say directly, *"Yes, I am willing"* or *"No, I am not willing."* Focusing on an ACOA's lack of involvement and apparent lack of commitment is not without its risks. Often it sets the stage for the person's leaving group. Some ACOAs are content merely to take up space. It allows them to claim that they are trying to get better while at the same time ensuring that their control and defenses remain intact. It is very easy for the rest of the group to become accomplices in that process.

"So Lynn, how's your recovery going?" She realized that something was going on because no one had been that direct with her before. She gave her standard line, *"I'm trying. I see how good you guys are doing and I wonder if I will ever be able to do it. When I try to talk I still get scared."* She was then asked, *"What are you doing to try to change that?"* She looked as if the question were in a foreign language. She didn't think it was her responsibility to do anything. A trace of anger began to show.

Other members began to share their experiences. *"When I was stuck in group, I decided to go to five self-help meetings a week." "When I felt that I didn't belong, I made a commitment to make daily phone calls to group members." "I realized that I wasn't talking about my life in group, so I kept a journal and reviewed it twice a week with a friend from group."* These suggestions were hard for Lynn to hear because they involved personal responsibility.

Lynn's problem with personal responsibility did not mean she was irresponsible in the usual sense. She was scrupulously responsible in social obligations, professional activities, and "cash register" honesty. Her responsibility covered the area of **doing** things. She had a blind spot regarding **personal responsibility in intimate relationships.** She did not take responsibility for extending and opening her inner self. She had no notion of joining with others. The other members were getting excited talking among themselves about what they did to benefit from group. While they were following that topic, Lynn withdrew, hoping the discussion wouldn't turn back to her. Eventually it did and people began to get angry. They began to understand they had "fallen for" and participated in her defenses. They realized they had viewed her as a pleasant afterthought. Lynn had presented as someone so fragile that they had left her alone.

Someone asked, *"After listening to us, have you decided on what you're going to do?"* This question demanded a response. It had shifted the entire focus. Previously Lynn was viewed as having an internal struggle and being resistant within herself. Now it began to become apparent that she was resisting the group members as well. There was a slight tone of defiance in her voice. *"I don't know what I'm going to do. I'm too afraid."* They asked her about meetings, *"Can you commit to going to five meetings per week?"* *"I don't know how many meetings I can get to"* was her response. *"Well, what about phone calls? Can you call one of us each day just to practice reaching out?"* Her response was *"I get nervous calling and I don't know what to say."*

As this process continued, Lynn got more angry. *"Why should I have to focus my whole life on this recovery stuff? What do you want from me?"* This is symptomatic of a core sense of rage. She had answered to and reached out to her alcoholic parents all her life. She was sick of having expectations placed on her. Now she was going to place the demands. It was the group's obligation to fix her and make her feel better. It was as if she believed her responsibility was to just attend group and then dare people to make her feel better. After spending her whole life dealing with the effects of alcoholism on her parents, she wanted to have somebody deal with her. She wanted people to take responsibility for her. She wasn't going to help them. They would have to guess and try various gambits with little, if any, help from her.

As a child of alcoholic parents, Lynn had spent her life adjusting to or complying with their unreasonable demands. The resultant anger was combined with a sense of entitlement. These self-defeating reactions were confronted by insistent healthy demands of her fellow group members. They wanted her to relate to and with them. She wanted to stay protected and be cured by magic. Lynn had been able to repress this conflict for two years. This core of rage had been camouflaged by an image of a sincerely sweet, but timid woman. She attempted to finesse her reluctance to make a commitment to her own recovery. She said, *"I would like to but I can't. I'm too afraid."* The reality was quite different. *I shouldn't have to and I won't."* The "I shouldn't have to" provided the key.

Lynn viewed making phone calls and going to meetings as punishment. Her statement, *"Why should I have to do all of that? I'm not the alcoholic"* also revealed the depth of her anger toward her parents. (This self-righteousness is also found in many spouses of alcoholics and can be viewed as a major factor in their illness.) The more she was pressed to act on her own behalf, the more angry and bratty she became. This was a side of her group had never seen. She was usually smiling or crying. Lynn was so threatened by this side of herself that she overcompensated with sweetness. Intuiting that her surface facade was fragile, she usually avoided interactions in group. The fear she presented was real, but it was misplaced. The fear was not about being unable to do things right in group. **The fear was that her camouflage would be seen through and her rage revealed.** This was an instance in which crying and being afraid were actually a way of maintaining control. It was safer to allow people to view her as sweet, but timid and fumbling, than to risk the rage and self-righteousness being exposed. *"I don't know why I'm so afraid of meetings"* masked *"I shouldn't have to go."*

This confrontation had to occur. Having the situation continue unchallenged would have done neither Lynn nor the group any good. A choice was called for. Not only would Lynn have to decide what she wanted to give to recovery but the group members also had to decide if they wanted to continue to be silent enablers of her inaction. ACOAs generally prefer to tolerate silently an obviously unhealthy situation. They hope to wait it out until the situation changes on its own. There is a fear of direct confrontation. They avoid conflict in the name of being accepting. However, Lynn was not truly accepted. The other group members formed an unspoken consensus to view her with a fond distance, neither giving nor asking much of her. To address this the therapist had to make a decision to bring the situation to a head.

Was there any way for Lynn to get out of the bind she was in? The answer can be viewed as the proverbial good news/bad news situation. The good news was that there were specific concrete actions that she could have taken which would have allowed her defenses to be lowered. She could have gone to daily meetings, made phone calls, and increased her socializing with group members. None of these steps would have required her to let go of her core defenses. It would not have mattered if she did these things out of spite, anger, or obstinacy. (*"I'll show them."*) The only thing that would have mattered was that she did them. That would have hopefully allowed the attractiveness of the spiritually based fellowships of AA and Al-Anon to slip under her defenses. If she could only have brought her body, eventually the mind would have followed.

The bad news was that since a direct request had finally been made of her, Lynn now viewed it as a fight. Through her anger she perceived that agreeing to the treatment plan would have been a humiliating surrender. There was no way she would do the very thing her parents should be doing. After all, **they** were the ones who needed help, **they** were the ones who had screwed up her life. Let **them** go to meetings! To have given in and made a major commitment to the recovery process would have necessitated Lynn's relinquishing the moral high ground that she had tenaciously climbed.

It is important that discovering the anger and hostility behind Lynn's sweetness not be viewed as an end point. It would have been very easy to have stopped there. But if the group members did, they would have been missed the central issue. Just as her sweetness was a defense against the anger and hostility she felt, the anger and hostility also served as a defense. As long as she could focus on being angry and feeling superior to her parents, she did not have to experience the enormity of the pain and trauma she had experienced as a child. She would fight having her anger exposed, but she would resist, almost at any cost, exposing how badly she had been hurt. The fight wasn't between Lynn and group members. It was between Lynn and her sense that she would be overwhelmed with anguish if she gave herself to this process.

The one thing that might have saved her is the tendency of ACOAs to want to follow rules and do things correctly. Pleasing others can be used to some therapeutic advantage. This was an instance in which behavioral change is primary to insight. The key would be for Lynn to act her way into openness. For whatever reason, if she began to go to daily meetings, made daily phone calls to group members, and had frequent social contacts with them, a transformation might have occurred. Openness might have grabbed her by surprise. The spiritual healing found at meetings might have rubbed off on her. At least she would have been taking frequent positive action on her own behalf. The self-revelation and exploration would come later as a by-product of those actions.

Unfortunately for many people like Lynn, it is asking more

than they can do. They have been so damaged and their pathologies are so entrenched they would leave group rather than face the possibility of uncovering too much. In one sense they have never joined group to begin with. When more is asked of them, it creates a crisis. Sharing more with the others involves sharing more of yourself. Some ACOAs do not have the ego structure to handle that. For some ACOAs the familiarity of surface relationships is perceived as safer than the interaction required by intimate relationships. In *Resistance and Recovery for Adult Children of Alcoholics,*[1] I explored whether in-depth recovery was possible for every ACOA. I believe some ACOAs have been so damaged that an internal transformation resulting in self-acceptance and intimacy with others is unlikely. For those ACOAs, progress can be made and improvement attained thereby reducing stress in their daily lives. The quality of their lives can be increased, but it is doubtful whether the nature of their relationships and self-concept can be changed. They can gain improvement yet transformation remains elusive.

SUMMARY POINTS

1. AN ACOA'S ACTS OF RESISTANCE AND REJECTION ARE MORE LIKELY TO BE OVERLOOKED WHEN THEY MANIFEST THEMSELVES IN A PLEASANT MANNER. The group becomes comfortable, almost enamoured, with this style of defense, and as a result is reluctant to be perceived as overbearing. This comfortability is often the enemy of recovery. The ACOA who is pleasantly resisting does not get the benefit of having healthy expectations placed on her. The other group members remain stuck in viewing confrontation as an attack, or a last-ditch reaction to hostile behavior, as opposed to a natural process in the give and take of attempting to structure a relationship.

2. CRYING AND FOCUSING ON BEING AFRAID CAN BE USED BY ACOAS TO MAINTAIN CONTROL. In this case, Lynn's tearfully expressed desire to belong served as a substitute for taking the steps necessary to join in community. **Many**

---

[1] Continuum, 1991.

ACOAs are caught in a dilemma of yearning to have intimate relationships while at the same time being terrified of actually obtaining them. In this case, Lynn attempted a compromise by attending group and showing her fear, which gave her a superficial connection with others. The result was that people treated her kindly, occasionally showing gentle concern. She belonged enough for people to like her, but not enough so that they would ask anything of her. She had the appearance of a relationship without the intimacy of one.

3. AN ACOA'S FEAR OF REVEALING HERSELF TO OTHERS OFTEN REFLECTS THE FEAR OF SEEING HERSELF AS SHE IS. It would have been incomplete to view Lynn's fear solely as an interpersonal problem. Trying to improve her communication and social skills while pointing out how much people wanted to help her would not have been enough. The real struggle was between Lynn and herself. She had to come to grips with who she was and the feelings she had. She had to become aware of and accept herself. Being in community with others and going to meetings would only serve as a supportive framework in which her internal activity could take place.

10

Going Out to Dinner

Just as group was about to start, Nora jumped in and said *"Before we begin, I was wondering if we could change the way we decide to go out to dinner."* The members had developed a tradition of going out to dinner after group. Nora continued, *"I think we waste time trying to figure out where we should go. Maybe we could set up a system where each week a different person gets to pick the restaurant."*

This seemingly casual request set off a chain reaction. Mary jumped in, *"I think it's wasting valuable time talking about this in group."* Lois was next, *"I agree with Mary. It makes me mad that we are talking about this in group."* Silence reigned and the tension could be cut with a knife. Nora gathered her courage and said, *"Lois, it scares me to say this and I know you're going to get mad, but I have to tell you that you scared me at dinner last week when you were dissatisfied with your food and sent it back."* Nora then pointed out how Lois seemed really angry and was muttering to herself during the meal. She thought Lois was overreacting.

Lois, who was mad at Nora for bringing the topic up in general, was even madder because it became focused on her. In addition to the anger, she felt fear as well. She had a vague sense of dread. She got defensive and started to justify her actions. *"I paid good money for that food and I have a right to get good food for my money."* Group members then attempted to critique Lois's restaurant style and defuse the tension. Ed said, *"Well, I think she did it right. She told the waiter what was wrong and insisted on getting it straight."* John said, *"I admire Lois. I wish I had the nerve to do that."* Dan said, *"Well my tendency is to have peace at any cost. I don't like rocking the boat."*

Nora was crying, and the group started to sound like an Emily Post seminar. Nobody knew what to do next. For such a seemingly innocent topic there was a lot of emotion and anxiety. They decided to explore what they were thinking and feeling at the restaurant.

Nora was upset because the scene at the restaurant triggered numerous memories of dinnertime with her alcoholic parents when she was a child. She was always afraid of a drunken explosion or fight. Her parents would fight over the quality of the meal or what was being served. Her job was to defuse the tension and try to forestall the fight. When her efforts failed, she would be terrified and try to withdraw into herself. She realized that even if Lois were polite and gracious about sending the food back, she not only would be tense and afraid but embarrassed as well. Sending the food back was more than a business transaction. Nora was afraid it would be taken as a comment on the personal worth of the waiter, cook, and even the busboy. She also expected the waiter to explode and yell at Lois if she made the request. She would have preferred that Lois just keep quiet and let it pass.

Lois was asked to explore what was going on inside of her prior to her sending the food back. It turned out she was angry to begin with because she didn't want to go to that restaurant. As soon as the food was served, she knew it was overcooked and she became angry, scared, and confused. *"Maybe I should just eat it and not make a big deal. If I send it back the others will be done with their meals before I even start mine. What if the waiter disagrees with me and says it's cooked properly?"* As her fear grew her anger intensified. Actually sending the food back was the culmination of a ten-minute internalized mounting rage. *"I'll show them. Who do they think they are? I work hard for my money."* Lois had to develop a rage in order to make a simple request. Saying she was not happy with a product became transformed into a primal act wrought with emotion.

Everyone at the table noted Lois's volcano getting ready to erupt. No one was able to address it directly. They tried to put it out of their minds. The unspoken consensus was to ignore it and make believe everything was fine. They hoped that they could eat fast enough to be done with the meal before the eruption happened. A couple of brave souls tried to distract Lois indirectly, but these efforts were more instinctive than conscious. After leaving the restaurant, they regarded the incident as closed (if they even thought about it) and having no importance.

Despite group members' initial displeasure at Nora for "wasting time," they soon discovered that it was significant. They realized that their reactions to the incident revealed major themes of how their ACOA syndrome dictated their interactions with others.

Those who got angry with her for making a fuss realized that they prided themselves on "making do" and not complaining. That pride leads to a subtle sense of superiority. *"Don't be a baby and complain over such a small thing. I've endured even worse and you don't see me complaining."* Feeling emotions interferes with what they have to accomplish. They viewed Lois's complaint as ruining their good time. **A good time is often defined as an absence of conflict.** Their background as children of alcoholics taught them that they never know when a minor request or complaint will result in an explosion; it is better to keep quiet and try to enjoy what has been handed to you. Complaining will only make things worse.

Others kept on trying to take care of Lois. Their happiness depended on everyone getting along. Anger, unhappiness, and disagreements are viewed as threats. They find it hard to believe that relationships can be based on being honest and expressing emotion during the give and take of daily living. As a result, they rarely do confront a situation directly. They try to divert someone who is getting angry in such a manner that the person is unaware of being diverted. This requires a keenly developed **hypervigilence** to inform them of potential conflict. They expend enormous energy in trying to manage what is not their problem to begin with.

Children of alcoholics develop this reaction for two reasons. First is self-protection. It is important to get a reading on their parents' moods so they can protect themselves by acting accordingly. Second is their desperation to see their parents stop fighting with each other and/or with them. Children of alcoholics will try many things to divert these overtly threatening fights and to maintain a false sense of calm.

Finally, there were those who tried to ignore the whole situation. They punched their "numb button" and tuned out until the incident was over. They repressed any anxiety or other emotion in order to regain a bland sense of equilibrium. There was a lack of connection, not only with others, but with their internal selves. They were frightened into inactivity. *"It never occurred to me to think anything about it."* Most often their interactions are primarily defensive, with silence being their main tool when faced with conflict.

It is important to note that these ACOAs have replicated their methods of interaction at the restaurant during the therapy group. All were scared, some blanked out, others attempted to rescue, some got mad at the peace being disturbed, and a couple had to simmer before they said anything. On a more fundamental level, **the restaurant and group gave them the opportunity to reveal and act out self-defeating themes established in childhood as a response to parental alcoholism.** That is why the primary task of ACOA group therapy is to provide the members with the opportunity to develop healthy, intimate relationships with each other. These relationships are based on their being honest, open, vulnerable, and by expressing their needs and setting limits. By actually having relationships, they can experience the barriers and obstacles that arise as they try to attain intimacy.

Problem solving is of minor value and can often hide opportunities for exploration and growth. The group members have a tendency to prefer problem solving. It is perceived as safer than being honest with another person about what you see in him and how it makes you feel. In this case it was not merely a question of developing decision-making skills in picking a restaurant or the proper manner of sending food back. Nor was it about the taking of sides and arguing who was right or who was wrong. It quickly became obvious that there was a reservoir of emotion which came up in the restaurant when Lois sent the food back and in group when Nora brought up the topic. Long-standing emotional reactions and barriers were present. It is the exploration of these reactions and barriers that sets the stage for recovery.

In exploring this event and their reaction to it, these ACOAs embraced the healing process. Many exciting things were accomplished. The group members addressed a fearful incident that they could easily have avoided. They shared a universal difficulty of ACOAs in appropriately expressing dissatisfaction. They attempted to create a process of decision making to replace one that was not working. Most importantly, they talked to each other about themselves and each other. They chose openness and vulnerability and didn't play it safe. Each time that their instincts told them to stop and retreat, their faith encouraged them to explore further.

Their journey took them from an incident in a restaurant to shared experiences at dinner tables in alcoholic families to how they react in relationships in general. Finally they arrived at how they act with each other. Doing so allowed each individual to increase his self-awareness and self-acceptance by talking about what was previously considered unmentionable and as a result realizing he wasn't alone.

SUMMARY POINTS

1. ACOAS OFTEN FIND INTELLECTUALIZING AND PROBLEM SOLVING SAFER THAN AN HONEST EXCHANGE OF FEELINGS AND PERCEPTIONS. It is easier to critique than search for meaning. ACOAs tend to use theoretical constructs to avoid vulnerability. This is part of their search for "correct" responses that address a problem and yet allow for a little vulnerability. It is safer to deal with a situation than with each other.

2. RITUALS AROUND MEALS ARE OFTEN SOURCES OF DIFFICULTY FOR ACOAS. Mealtime in alcoholic families is a time of unpredictability with a potential for disaster. Most of the components of a very volatile mixture are present. The question is whether anything will cause these components to ignite during a given meal. A child can only guess what will cause a spark. A parent might be drunker than usual, a sarcastic remark may be taken as a challenge, or somebody would appear to be too happy. This creates an atmosphere of tension. It is not surprising that ACOAs are susceptible to eating disorders.

3. BEING ASSERTIVE IS OFTEN VIEWED BY ACOAS AS A DECLARATION OF WAR OR AN ATTACK. As a result AOCAs are often embarrassed over the reasonable attempts of others to express dissatisfaction. Taking positive action on their own behalf is outside of their normal activity. Expressing dissatisfaction is usually preceded by a buildup of anger and indig-

nation combined with fear and doubt. They approach the situation believing they will be ignored, humiliated, or attacked. To compensate for that fear, they marshal all of their resources into an emotional response that is out of proportion to the requirements of the situation.

4. ACOAS COMBINE HYPERVIGILENCE WITH SELF-CEN-SORSHIP. This allows them to be aware of tension and conflict, but gives them no healthy means of addressing it. These insights were not designed to bring them closer to people. The original purpose of these traits was to help AOCAs keep their distance from the chaos that surrounded them. These traits allowed ACOAs to manipulate the people in their lives in order to create a safe, secure spot for themselves. As a result ACOAs can usually read a person's mood and give an appropriate response. The task of ACOAs in recovery is to use this insight into others to increase, rather than limit, what they can reveal of themselves. Hopefully they will recognize their common bonds.

5. AN ACOA'S INTERACTION OUTSIDE OF GROUP IS MIRRORED BY HIS BEHAVIOR IN GROUP. Nothing that happens is too insignificant to discuss in group. There is something to be discovered in each interaction AOCAs have with each other. One of the advantages of being in a group with people from the same background is that it is easy to see similar themes and patterns. It is very useful to be able to trace unhealthy methods of interacting back to their roots in the alcoholic family and the subsequent defenses that developed.

11

Go Away, I Already Gave

Martha was the youngest member of her ACOA group. As a result it was easy for group members not to ask too much of her. Most of the time that suited Martha just fine. She looked and dressed rather plainly. She would preface most of her statements with a self-deprecating remark. She never took the lead and would often appear to have faded into the woodwork. It was not that Martha attempted to portray a particular image. Instead she conveyed the impression that she had no image at all, with little to offer others.

Her presentation was deceptive because there was more to her than the image she presented. Every now and then members would get a glimpse of a very quick, hot temper. This anger was rarely expressed directly. Instead, it would seep out in the form of intense "if looks could kill" glares or sarcastic dismissals.

One member who was frequently driven home by Martha was finally able to express how scared she was about one particular manifestation of Martha's transformed anger. Martha drove like a mad woman. She would get behind the wheel of her car and become "Sherman marching through Georgia," speeding and cursing anyone or anything that got in her way. Martha, after much probing, admitted that she had gotten speeding tickets coming home from group and was in danger of loosing her license. The anger and other emotions that she generated, but did not express in group, were played out on the highway. It was a high and dangerous price to pay for her ongoing repression of anger.

When she talked in group Martha sounded like someone who was helpless and overwhelmed. She gave the impression that she had nothing to offer. However, on occasion, the group got the sense that she was more substantial than her image suggested. As time went on and Martha revealed more of her story, it was readily apparent that reality was quite different from the impression she gave. Her actions throughout her life revealed her as an extraordinarily capable and competent person.

So far during her life she had taken care of a sick brother who suffered from a terminal illness, was responsible for nursing her mother as her death approached, and had to deal with an alcoholic father who expected her to do everything for him. As a volunteer, she handled the administrative details of her parish. At work, even though she had no formal authority and received a very low wage, she was invaluable to her boss. When she would talk about these events she would become very guarded and devoid of emotion. She would belittle her accomplishments and their emotional cost. She would sketch the barest outlines and then shut off any discussion or explanation.

Martha had a mixture of two traits commonly found in ACOAs, a profound sense of inferiority, coexisting with excellent organizational and caretaking skills. She was forced to develop the ability to take care of her family members and to manage a household because her parents' alcoholism placed the burden on her. She had to step in and fulfill the function of her parents. Parental alcoholism, which forced these caretaking skills to develop, also forced the sense of inferiority to grow. As the alcoholism progressed, the situation deteriorated. Martha's extraordinary efforts could only slow the disintegration. With no external validation or perspective, she viewed herself as a failure because she could not achieve the goal she had set for herself, namely to save her family.

It was as if she were daring group to feel sorry for her. Her internal rage would be transformed into hostility toward the people who were trying to care for her. The more group would reach out to her, the more she would dismiss them. *"It's really no big deal." "So what, that's in the past."* In the beginning, there would actually be fights. Martha would trivialize the tragedies in her life; members would try to get her to acknowledge the pain; Martha would then dismiss them with a cutting remark and be angry; and finally members would get mad and try even harder. Both sides got locked into a dance of seeking and moving away.

Finally the answer appeared. Group members decided to resign from the dance. They reached a consensus not to fight with her anymore. As one member said, *"There isn't anything you can do to make me stop caring for you. If you want to keep everything inside, fine. I won't try to pull it out of you. However, I want you to know that I care for you."* Then came the kicker that would set the tone for later growth. *"Also there is nothing you can do for me."* It is important to note that this was not said in anger or out of spite. It was a resignation from an unhealthy method of interaction. It was not the abandoning of a friend. Martha was issued an invitation rather than a rejection. No longer would they wordlessly dance, ignoring what was happening between them.

This brought out the effectiveness of the ACOA group. In the past Martha's defenses were very effective. They succeeded in protecting her emotions, ending discussion, and precluding any exploration of herself or her situation. These defenses, when used in the context of an ACOA group, served to reveal that she was troubled. Being so incongruous to the atmosphere of caring in the group, they served as red flags, marking an area of emotional conflict. Group members did not withdraw and leave her alone. They made her aware of her defenses which then forced her to stay with and experience her discomfort. The defenses, which served to protect Martha from the members of her alcoholic family by keeping them away, now became the key which allowed group members into her life.

This approach was different. Martha felt totally disarmed. No one had ever treated her with such a combination of gentleness and firmness. Not only did people say they weren't going to fight with her, they also said that their care wasn't predicated on her performance. She had never experienced people wanting nothing **from** her but everything **for** her. Such caring was stifled by alcoholism. This is not to say that alcoholic parents wouldn't give anything to feel that way. It's just that this disease not only robs them but also takes away their ability to see something is missing.

The group, though unconditionally affirming her, would not be a doormat. Not fighting with her did not mean they would let her sarcastic glances go by without comment. They simply weren't going to interact with her based on the unhealthy rules developed as a result of alcoholism. She would be free to stay in her own misery. When she wanted to open herself to them, they would accept her. It was her choice.

Martha had no self-worth because she had never experienced

unconditional nurturing from the significant people in her life. The primary people in her life acted as **unquenchable takers.** Her job was to give and keep giving. She believed she was tolerated based on her performance. If only she could do enough, her parents would see the light and affirm her. That affirmation never came. Instead her efforts only brought more demands. That is why it was so important when she was told that she could do nothing to earn the group's caring. It was a gift.

Martha wasn't conscious that her experiences were out of the ordinary. She was unable to see that unreasonable demands were placed on her by her family. As a child she had no means to protect herself from the very people who should have been protecting her to begin with. She was placed in the dilemma of defining herself by what she did while never being able to do enough. The demands always escalated, but she never got anything back in return. At some level, she must have had the instinct, *"If I appear helpless, no one will ask anything of me."* Her image of inability and helplessness was her response to the continuous, unreasonable, and unfulfillable demands placed on her by the people she loved. It's no wonder she looked and talked the way she did.

The emotions and trauma she had to address were fairly straightforward and unsophisticated. They were not disguised or transformed to the point that they were difficult to recognize. In one sense that made them easier to deal with. All she had to do was trust enough and begin to speak. Silence was her worst enemy. If she would talk, the problem areas would reveal themselves naturally and begin to dissipate. Contrary to her appearance and manner, Martha's silence was not a function of fear. It was more a function of her anger. It could best be described as an attacking silence. It was directed *at* people rather than *from* them. That explained the hostility that group members detected.

The greatest gift the group gave Martha was wanting nothing from her. Not having to be consumed by the perceived, unreasonable demands of her fellow group members freed Martha. *"Maybe these people really are different."* The first change after the "no fight declaration" was that she came to group with a different haircut and a new outfit. The difference was startling. One person said, *"You look like a woman rather than a girl!"* She received an ovation. The praise, compliments, and applause were almost painful for her to experience. On the surface she made a halfhearted effort to shrug it off, but it was obvious that she was reveling in it and yearning for it to continue. Upon seeing this everyone decided to keep praising her. Not only was she getting what she had always dreamed of, but people noticed that she liked it and gave her more.

This set the stage for Martha's next step. She began to talk. Talking, secure in her acceptance by the group, she began to experience and release the stored up pain and anger. She was amazed how smooth and natural it seemed once she started. Though making progress, she found it much easier to talk about the past rather than the present. She knew that members would accept her past unconditionally. Regarding the present, she still had vestiges of the fear. She was afraid that they would make demands or try to control her. Even worse, she believed she would be unable to meet those demands and have everything she had gained taken from her.

This barrier was approached when she was able to talk about her new boyfriend. She brought it up with great trepidation. Martha was afraid group members would criticize her and tell her she wasn't ready for a romantic relationship. Martha herself was unsure and realized that both she and her boyfriend had problems to work out. She did know that she really liked him and wanted to try. In her mind, the stage was set for war. A tiny thing happened that was monumental. Martha was able to be open and honest about what she was thinking. She was able to tell group she was starting to view them as adversaries. Once she spoke about her suspicion and hostility she then grasped that the relationship between her and her boyfriend was not the main topic. The main issue was the relationship between her and group.

By sharing her fear of them and how she came in prepared to do battle, she touched a universal theme. Her honesty and openness invited the other ACOAs to do the same thing. Martha shared with group members how they turned in her eyes from caring friends into enemies intent on depriving or controlling her. She was afraid her fears would be confirmed and she would be judged harshly with no recourse. It was a testament to her recovery that Martha had developed such a sense of self that she could invite the others to explore themselves and find their common humanity.

Eventually the discussion came back to Martha and her boyfriend. The group surprised her. People were very supportive. They encouraged her to try out the relatiotionship and have fun. They told her that no romance is devoid of problems. She learned that mood swings were very common in the early stages of getting to know someone. Instead of fighting with her, Martha discovered the group members had a wealth of information they wanted to share with her. They were more enthusiastic than she was. Their reaction could best be summed up as, *"We forbid you to break up with him for at least two months. You owe it to yourself to see if this romance is real, so we command you to give it your best shot. Just keep in touch so we can help."*

All of the internal changes led to a major external change in her life. Martha decided to go back to college. The process she used to arrive at this decision is more important than the decision itself. She came to the decision in community with others. At first she thought it might be a good idea to take one night course at a community college. She viewed it as a major step and was scared. As usual with Martha, there was more present than what met the eye.

People to this day still talk about the night she brought in her transcript from her first try at going to college. They were expecting some failures and the rest of the grades to be almost average. What kind of marks did this heretofore, helpless and hopeless girl have? Dean's list! Despite the fact she was going to school and nursing her dying mother at the same time, she did great. That night she also revealed that her high school grades were extremely high. When her principal told her she was top in her class and was going to be the valedictorian she panicked. She didn't think she could speak in public, so she believed her only way out was to lower her grades. This resulted in her graduating number three in her class rather than number one. It never occurred to her to ask for help. Even though there was no one at home to help her, there might have been some support at school.

It all revolved around a lack of self-worth. *"Who am I to speak at graduation?"* Knowing this, the group wondered whether she wasn't selling herself short by only taking one course at a community college. *"Why not enroll full-time at a four-year school?"* It had never occurred to her that she could be accepted in a four-year school and be able to do the work. On another level it never dawned on her that she deserved to go to school as a full-time student. She did not view herself as worthy to focus completely on studies and experience the advantages of college life. She had little, if any, sense that a college degree would change her life. She just assumed she would return to the same dead-end job upon completion. Once college was over, she was afraid she would be the same person, stuck in the same place, with the only difference being she would have more debt.

The end result was that with the group's encouragement she explored these issues and decided to go to a four year school. She applied, got accepted, arranged financing and housing, and began her course of study all within three months. Throughout this process she was helped by group members who had various areas of expertise. This was in stark contrast to her previous history of self-sufficiency and doing for others.

Martha still had some difficulty in picking a major. It was hard for her to view herself worthy of a high-paying, responsible, executive position. This represented a curious paradox. Though she might sometimes view herself as incapable, heaven help anyone else who would even hint at it. **Even though she tended to put herself down first in order to forestall anyone else, she also had a core belief that she had superior capabilities.** She had two different measuring sticks. Compared to how she viewed others, she felt superior, but compared to how she judged herself, by her own standards, she felt inferior. This was a more advanced issue that would play itself out as her recovery progressed. She was safely in an environment in which she could freely assess her strengths and weaknesses, while at the same time be secure in the acceptance of her fellow ACOAs.

SUMMARY POINTS

1. TRANSFORMATION HAPPENED WHEN MARTHA WAS ABLE TO ACCEPT THE GROUP AS PROVIDING A CARING ALTERNATIVE TO THE UNREASONABLE DEMANDS THAT HAD PREVIOUSLY CHARACTERIZED HER LIFE. She was able to see herself as they viewed her and was freed from viewing herself through her own defenses and misperceptions. By refusing to fight, they gave her nothing to react against. **She was able to see that her main defenses depended on the unhealthy**

reaction of others in order to be perpetuated. Faced with a healthy reaction of honest and open limit setting combined with acceptance, Martha was forced to come face to face with herself.

2. ONCE THE INVITATION TO BELONG WAS ACCEPTED, NO IN-DEPTH ANALYSIS WAS NEEDED. Martha saw that her pathetic image was no longer necessary. She learned that it was better to refuse an unreasonable demand directly than to adopt a helpless image in hopes that it wouldn't be made. Though acting helpless cut down on some demands placed on her, it also cut down on the avenues open to her. She sacrificed more and more opportunities in order to preserve the image.

3. IN TRYING TO MAKE A DECISION REGARDING A ROMANCE, MANY ACOAS FEAR THAT OTHER PEOPLE WILL EXPRESS THE SAME DOUBTS THAT THEY HAVE, BUT ARE AFRAID TO FACE. These doubts grow and get transformed from concern about a romance to doubt about one's self worth. As a result, openness decreases and is replaced with an evasiveness designed to give the appearance of exploration while actually preserving the status quo.

4. MARTHA'S DECISION TO GO TO COLLEGE WAS OBJECTIVELY NEUTRAL; HOW IT WAS MADE AND WHAT IT REPRESENTED WAS CRUCIAL. If she had decided that college would create a sense of self and prove she wasn't as bad as she thought, then it would not have been of much value. If she made all the arrangements on her own in order to prove her competence, it would not have advanced her recovery. In this case, college was of primary value because it allowed Martha to explore herself and to act in community with others on her own behalf. College was only a by-product of Martha's discovering herself.

12

The Graduate

Keith "graduated" from group. During his five years in group he had grown enormously. He had accomplished a great deal. He had come to believe in himself and embrace both his strengths and weaknesses. He had truly joined in community with others. When he first came to group he was very guarded and filled with fear. He was leading a solitary life with no sense of belonging or purpose. Now his life was rich and full. He belonged to a community that was based on mutual caring and support. By trusting and depending on others he became free to trust and depend on himself.

This is not to say that he was "fixed." He still had problems and difficulties. The difference was that he had developed the resources to face the problems and difficulties of life in an open and healthy manner. Keith had a sense of self-love and self-acceptance. He was able to see and embrace reality. His relationships with others were characterized by a deepening intimacy. When he first came to group it took a great deal of effort and emotional energy for him to simply get through each day. At the end of his time in group, he was amazed at how effortless his life seemed.

Keith had a beautiful seven-month departure process. It began when he shared his first inklings that it might be near the time for him to leave. This commitment to openness allowed others to share in the process. It became a joint venture rather than a solitary journey. This was a critical step. By sharing this process from the start, Keith created a framework for exploration. Within this framework both Keith and the other members were free to take the necessary steps to ensure that Keith's departure would strengthen their relationship instead of end it. This was a major step for someone from an alcoholic family.

ACOAs do not handle separation well. It is preferable to quietly slip away rather than face the emotions generated by a loved one's departure. Rarely is an imminent departure addressed in an open, direct manner. To do so would mean that ACOAs would have to talk openly about what a person meant to them. Hope, fear, and confusion are present in the departure of a loved one. These are emotions that do not get openly discussed in alcoholic families. As a result, ACOAs tend to make snap announcements of decisions to leave or accept without question (while hiding their true feelings) someone else's departure. They view separation as the ending of a relationship. They have little, if any, experience of the fact that sharing openly the joy and sorrow of separation solidifies and enriches a relationship.

It would be unrealistic to think that there weren't times when Keith tried to forget that his time in group was coming to an end. He had to resist the tendency to coast and just fade away. However, when these tendencies occurred, either he would catch himself or the group members would point out what was happening. This process could not be more different from what happens in an alcoholic family. It involved shared decision making and planning ahead with confidence in the future. Group members helped and supported each other while preparing for Keith's departure. They shared the joys and pain experienced along the way. These shared anticipations and preparations are among the things alcoholism robs from families.

Keith worked very hard the last two months he was in group. Originally he had only been aware of fear and apprehension about leaving. It made sense because a deep bond had developed during the five years. *"What will I do once I leave?"* *"Will I stay friends with you after I'm gone?"* *"Will people forget me?"* These questions would have festered if he had kept them to himself. They would have shown up disguised as withdrawal or hostility. In sharing them, Keith became free. He discovered that other members had similar thoughts but were afraid to express them. They thought it might depress him or make him believe he shouldn't go. Even better than providing relief, sharing his thoughts paved the way for his recognition of the happiness he was feeling. He no longer had to squander his emotional energy, repressing those fearful thoughts and feelings. No longer compelled to rigidly attempt to be perfect, he was free to discover that not only was he happy, but he had a sense of pride and wonder. He saw that there was much more to him than his fear.

For the first time in his life, Keith was anticipating and planning for a major event. In his eyes this was the most important occasion of his life. He was actually allowing himself to become excited. Growing up in an alcoholic family forced him not to anticipate pleasurable events because they often failed to occur (e.g., because of blackouts) or were disastrous if they did occur (e.g. intoxication). Now he wanted to celebrate this major accomplishment. Keith was also fully aware that it wasn't just **his** accomplishment. Everyone could see that they had entered his life and touched him in depth. It was a shared accomplishment.

Keith's sharing the process of his departure was a gift to the group. It gave them the opportunity to explore, not only how they reacted to someone's leaving but also how they reacted to someone achieving "graduation" before them. At first everyone was uniformly happy for him. *"You're a great guy and you deserve it." "You worked hard for this." "The change in you is inspiring." "This gives me hope that my time will come."* Although these thoughts and feelings were true, they only told part of the story. Actually the members had greatly mixed emotions, but they were afraid to express them. They thought that they had to support Keith. To feel or express anything other than happiness would be considered selfish and would run the risk of spoiling it for him.

The bond they felt for Keith and the sense of trust they had developed allowed them to explore and share their true thoughts and feelings. There was a general sadness and sense of loss. People had begun to look to Keith as a leader they could count on to lead the charge into fearful areas. Not only did they wonder who would take his place, they were fearful that they would be called upon to do more in group. Others were jealous. It took great courage for one to say, *"I wish it were me instead of you."*

There was also some discouragement. Some wondered if they would ever be ready to leave. They could see no end in sight for themselves. A good deal of anger came to the surface. People were mad that they had to be in group to begin with. (This was especially true for those who were the only ones in their family to be in treatment.) Some anger was even directed at Keith. *"I don't think you're ready to leave." "I wouldn't have picked you as being ready to leave."*

It was safe to assume that all of these "negative" feelings were rampant among the group members. Rather than being indicators of selfishness, all of these expressed thoughts and feelings were testaments to the health of the group. It showed their level of trust and commitment to each other. They were able to risk revealing these "dark and bad" thoughts to somebody that they loved. By breaking through their tendencies toward self-censorship and giving a correct response, they were able to be vulnerable both with Keith and each other. They weren't alone with their thoughts and feelings. **Even Keith had similar thoughts, but denied them because he thought they meant he really wasn't ready to graduate.** Instead of harming their relationship with Keith, being honest strengthened it and made it richer. It was a great going away present.

In a healthy ACOA group the fact that **recovery means departure** is faced openly and together. It is not ignored until the last minute.

ACOAs are particularly vulnerable in the areas of loss and abandonment. Often they begin to prepare for what they believe will be an inevitable loss or rejection immediately upon introduction. This is done by limiting how much they will invest in the relationship and minimizing how important a person is to them. In their eyes, separation means more than a painful departure. It is seen as an abrupt, total loss. It also means a greatly decreased likelihood of ever having another relationship. Themes regarding investment of self and future separations will always be present in an ACOA group. That is why the whole area of a member's departure must be periodically and actively addressed. Since all group members are (or should be) actively involved in twelve-step programs, it is difficult for them to grasp that the ACOA group will have an end point. It is not forever. In AA, Al-Anon, and ACOA twelve-step groups there is a leisurely concept of time and progress. It is generally expected that participation, though at various levels, be a lifelong process. In the therapy group there is an end point. Members work and make progress in order to be able to leave group in a healthy manner. This concept is different than the self-help groups. As a result, it is important to emphasize that a person's time in group has an end point, and when that point arrives it will mean changing the relationship with the other members.

In alcoholic families, the future is generally bleak. Change means getting worse. As the disease of alcoholism progresses, not only does the physical and emotional deterioration of the alcoholic continue but the family structure deteriorates as well. Today is worse than yesterday, but tomorrow (barring a miracle) will be worse than today. The key in that environment is to hold on to what you have because change is seen as a diminishment. That is why ACOA group members tend to think and hope that group membership will basically remain the same. A few peripheral members may come and go, but the basic core will remain the same. They believe if the core members change, the group will be hollow. There is no conception that new members could add to the group's value. The painful fact that must be realized is that the people the ACOAs have grown very close to will move on. This is just like life. Addressing this is very fruitful for the members.

ACOAs often limit closeness and deepening relationships in order to avoid feeling pain when a person leaves. Successful as this defense is in limiting pain, it also succeeds in limiting joy and happiness. In preparing to defend against a person's inevitable departure, ACOAs don't embrace that person's arrival. The question that should be asked is not *"Will I have a relationship with you after you leave group?"* The question instead should be *"Do I have a relationship with you now?"*

Keith's last group session gave the members a chance to express their feelings toward him **at that moment.** The members lived for the present moment and had faith that the future would take care of itself. This is not to say that they did not believe they had to actively pursue a relationship with Keith. Instead it signified that they believed the future would be positive. They believed everyone had goodwill, the resources to act on their own behalf, and were under the care of a "power greater than themselves." In short, they believed they were healthy and free from the shackles of alcoholism and no longer had to operate in a defensive manner.

In Keith's next individual session, he talked about how moving and beautiful his last group session was. It was a night he would always remember. After talking for fifteen minutes, he then moved on to other topics. Life continued. During the course of the next month he reported a series of seemingly unrelated, irritating, emotional brushfires. His girlfriend was making too many demands; people at work were not responding to his supervision, and his bosses weren't acting the way they should. He had recently bought a house and it increasingly became the center of his life. He had scheduled an overwhelming agenda of repairs for himself. He was becoming a man possessed by an obsessive attack of "This Old House" itis.

The more Keith talked, the more he was able to see that he was viewing people as a nuisance and a bother. He was exhibiting a minor return of an old narcissistic perspective. People existed only in terms of how they affected him, and that effect was generally negative. They were viewed as things to avoid or maneuver around. They became threats to a zealously guarded rigid schedule he had developed for himself. Socializing had become a burden rather than an opportunity. Phoning group members had fallen by the wayside. All he wanted was to be left alone so he could work on his house. *"It's important that this stuff gets done because I have deadlines to meet."* He also revealed that his home improvement efforts were primarily solitary projects undertaken on his own. There was no room for anyone to help. Keith's world was constricting piece by piece and he was so caught up that he couldn't see it happening.

As you can guess by now, all this coincided with his departure from group. The trauma of leaving brought about the re-emergence of his old defenses. This regression is common among people who successfully complete a major portion of therapy. It is as if the entire therapeutic process is telescoped into the post-departure period. During that time the person must rework his progress. The successful completion of this task results in its consolidation and internalization.

Keith's increased narcissism, his adversarial view of people, and his retreat into the safety of his own home were markedly different from the new manner of relating that had emerged over the past five years. Although this created some discomfort for him, it did not represent a setback. To use AA terms, it would be considered as a "slip." The reason for this "slip" was that he did not process his departure **after he left.** He believed that group was done once he left it. According to his way of thinking, it should have been over and no problems left once he walked out of the room.

This way of thinking is quite prevalent among ACOAs. Many have the attitude of *"The past is the past. Let's move on. There's no use crying over spilled milk."* Not wanting to look back, they believed their problems would be over once they left the traumatic situation. They did not realize that even though the situation was over, internal conflicts remained. Keith was not aware that he still had a lot of work to do regarding group.

Keith mistakenly thought that a sense of ongoing sorrow and loss contradicted his sense of joy and excitement. It would have indicated that he made a mistake in leaving. On his own he couldn't grasp that **it was natural for these feelings to exist side by side.** To protect against these feelings and any future losses, a protective shell began to emerge. Leaving his feelings of sadness and loss repressed in darkness and silence allowed his old "semi-retired" defenses to begin to sprout. Repressing painful feelings of loss necessitated his pulling back from people and socializing. Being with people caused aggravation. Each time he had contact with group members his unconscious pain was irritated. It made perfect sense that he withdrew into the safety of his house. There he could control his environment and have a sense of permanence through a series of never-ending repairs that required the total absorption of his energy. There would be no time left for him to feel lonely.

Keith was incredulous as this picture developed. *"How can this be? I haven't thought of group since I left! Isn't that odd?"* In the month that followed the most joyous day of his life, he hadn't paused to reflect or savor the event. It was his most significant accomplishment, yet he hadn't thought about it. Keith sheepishly said, *"I see what you mean."* He saw that he was treating the most important day of his life as if it never existed. However, the depth of his recovery was such that he remained open. The previous month crystallized for him and a sense of awareness came. He was then able to experience, as well as talk about, what he **really** felt as opposed to what he was **trying** to feel. Being able to talk and accepting the invitation to talk about all of his feelings were all he needed.

It took Keith a little over four weeks to get tired of his living situation and the reemergence of his old ways. That is in stark contrast to many ACOAs who can spend decades bearing the unbearable. Once he was ready to talk about the symptoms, he was ready to see their root cause. It was proof positive of his recovery. His "graduation" wasn't a fluke. He had internalized the love and caring of his fellow ACOAs and that, in turn, gave him an acceptance of self and sense of trust. This sense of self and trust enabled him to see reality. Relief was instantaneous. Keith could then recognize that he had lots of emotions about leaving. He understood that just because relationships changed didn't mean they had to end. Finally, he was able to work on his own behalf.

Instead of viewing himself as a victim of his own success, and wallowing in the loneliness of graduation, he could acknowledge it and then go on to actively work to re-create and restructure his friendships. He was able to see that not only had his friends from group become his major support system while he was in group, but they continued to be once he was out of group. Leaving group wasn't the end he thought it would be. It was actually the beginning.

SUMMARY POINTS

1. ACOAS FEAR OPEN, DIRECT, AND PROCESSED SEPARATIONS WITH PEOPLE THEY CARE FOR. The pain of separation arouses a deep sense that the person leaving is irreplaceable. This stems from the belief that the departure will create an emptiness that will never be filled. This is further complicated by an unconscious belief that filling that void would be a betrayal to the person who had left. Therefore, ACOAs use a variety of coping mechanisms (e.g., picking a fight, not addressing a departure, and joking) to avoid facing the pain of separation. Their task is to realize that separation as a result of a shared process can deepen a relationship through jointly exploring and sharing a significant and moving experience.

2. LIVING WITH ALCOHOLIC PARENTS MAKES IT DIFFICULT FOR CHILDREN TO DEVELOP A SENSE OF TRUST, EXCITEMENT, AND PREDICTABILITY ABOUT THE FUTURE. The future is viewed with fear and apprehension rather than joy and antic- ipation. Hope often comes from belief in an instantaneous

miracle or an external intervention that will stop the downward spiral or aimless emotional drifting. As a result, ACOAs act to protect and consolidate the relationships that already exist. They believe that if these relationships change or end, they may not be replaced. This is in contrast to the belief that a person's capacity to love increases the more a person loves. In guarding against projected pain of future departures, ACOAs limit the happiness of present relations.

3. THE SENSE OF TAKING ACTIVE STEPS FOR EVENTUAL GRADUATION FROM GROUP IS IMPORTANT FOR ACOAS. Although twelve-step group participation is essential, it is also different from the therapeutic process, especially in the area regarding length of stay. ACOA therapy group participation does end. This fact provides the framework to deal with such issues as relationships, commitment, hope, loss, and change. It is especially important in long-term, stable groups to bring this to people's attention on a regular basis.

Conclusions

The stories in this book have a diversity of detail and a commonality of themes. Together they give hints to the nature of recovery. ACOAs facing and embracing the reality of everyday experiences give rise to extraordinary levels of awareness and growth. The issues addressed in these stories are not spectacular. Their power lies in the fact that people from alcoholic families had to make such remarkable efforts in order to address them. The essence of an ACOAs recovery is finding the richness of the ordinary and accepting life on its own terms.

An author can never be sure what people will remember from a book. Here are some points to consider that I find compelling.

I. APPROPRIATE TREATMENT OF ACOAS REQUIRES A BLEND OF TRADITIONAL PSYCHODYNAMIC THERAPY, DIRECTIVE AL-COHOLISM COUNSELING, AND THE SPIRITUALITY OF GROUPS SUCH AS ALCOHOLICS ANONYMOUS AND AL-ANON. Working with ACOAs provides a marvelous opportunity to create a specific treatment approach which combines appropriate parts of these three proven approaches to helping people. It also provides therapists with the chance to move beyond the confines of one rigid school of thought.

Dan needed more than a directed approach to help him learn how to cope with his wife's vacation. Evan could analyze his sexual development and take concrete steps to share with others, yet he needed a conversion experience before he became vulnerable. Lois simply did not know how to date and all the insight in the world wouldn't provide those skills.

The key element in their success is that they, and their

counselors, were willing to go beyond preconceived notions and look for what worked. It is ironic to note that often ACOAs are seeking help in developing flexibility from some of the most inflexible people around.

2. RECOVERY IS TO BE FOUND THROUGH THE COMMON EVENTS OF LIFE. ACOAs often place themselves outside of the mainstream of life. A little bit of jargon can be dangerous. It is painful to see ACOAs creating and falling prey to a world which keeps them in the clutches of this syndrome. The language of this universe is composed of phrases and words such as: my lost child, the shame that binds, co-dependence, warm fuzzies, teddy bears, grief work, and healing my inner child.

Who really talks like that? Such talk is a satirist's dream come true. ACOAs need to learn to experience and accept life's give and take. Ken's trip to New York City was a disaster. So what! He could whine and immerse himself in psychobabble or listen and discover that most first trips with a new girlfriend include a huge fight as part of the itinerary.

The problem is not so much what happens in life. The problem is how ACOAs handle it. The birth of a child is always conflictual. Kay's problem was not with her husband and in-laws. It was with her own attitudes and perceptions. Joel could have simply stated he didn't feel comfortable enough to go out to dinner with group. Although that would have been disappointing, it was also understandable. It was his talk of brainwashing and programming that got him into so much conflict.

3. REALITY IS OFTEN HIDDEN BEHIND TRUTH. ACOAs often use surface details to camouflage deeper truth. Tom's talking about his uncle's death protected the impact of his uncle's life. Denise's talk of visiting her future in-law hid the fact that the woman was in a coma which then would have given rise to exposing her sense of guilt. Martha's presentations completely hid her academic achievements.

In each instance crucial details which would have given a truer picture of the person were covered or replaced with less revealing information. No one did this consciously. There was no intent to deceive. This defense's function is to allow ACOAs to maintain a sense of control. It prevents them from facing a part of themselves which would cause emotional turmoil if acknowledged.

Witnessing this defense often gives a person a sense of unease. The ACOA appears to be trying, yet something isn't quite right. Often it is difficult to identify what is wrong. It took a long time to wade through Lynn's reasons for not going to Al-Anon meetings. Each excuse she gave was accurate and valid, but the discomfort of group members grew. Finally, they were able to break through these facts and get to reality. She was enraged that she had to be the only one in her family getting help. As ACOAs progress in recovery they begin to realize that if they think there is something more to the information a person has given them, they generally are right.

4. ADDRESSING CONFLICT IS MORE IMPORTANT THAN AVOIDING IT. This indicates a switch on the part of ACOAs. As the recovery process progresses, they no longer view themselves as powerless people who must prevent conflict at any cost. They begin to realize that conflict is a part of life. Addressing it in an appropriate manner is usually beneficial to all parties.

In families with active alcoholism conflict was viewed as dangerous. If one or more people were drunk, conflict could quickly escalate to an all out verbal attack or even violence. Conflict was also dangerous since, if pursued, it would generally lead to an acknowledgment of alcoholism, the family secret. Instead of resolving a problem, conflict generally made it worse.

Group members, though afraid, felt confident to confront Lois about her behavior at the restaurant. People felt compelled to talk to her because they knew they would retreat from her if they did not. Confronting her not only affirmed their perceptions, but it affirmed Lois as well. They took a risk in showing her how she scared people and acted arrogant.

Not addressing conflict can damage a relationship. Keith's silent withdrawal was harmful. If he would have expressed his irritation to others a useful argument might have ensued. This could have allowed Keith to experience the consequences of his withdrawal and hopefully make some changes. His friends who watched him pull away weren't doing him a favor by keeping silent. If they would have taken an active interest in their relationship with Keith they could have helped him.

If a relationship can't tolerate appropriate honesty it may not be worth having. Evan couldn't continue in group unless he was honest. He wanted more affirmation than the group gave him. He was preparing to leave group rather than tell his friends he wanted more. He thought they would be as embarrassed of this request as he was. Until he was honest, he would keep pulling away.

5. ACOAS DEFENSES OFTEN REQUIRE OUTSIDE SUPPORT FOR THEIR MAINTENANCE. Most ACOAs defenses develop as a response to parental alcoholism. What is problematic in adulthood has it's roots in a child's reasonable attempts to cope with an unreasonable situation. The defenses are primarily reactive. Alcoholism can be viewed as an obstacle course children must navigate throughout their physical, emotional, and developmental growth. After decades of such a defensive approach to life, many ACOAs lose sight of their own needs and involve themselves with people they can react against.

Martha depended on group members fighting with her. They would suggest something and she in turn would say why it would not work. Her method of getting attention was to bring up a problem, dare people to help, rebuff their attempts, and then feel vindicated because people were always mad at her. Progress was impossible until group members refused to engage in the cycle. Only then was she able to look at herself.

Lynn depended on others viewing her as fragile. Members would be so solicitous of her that neither she nor they had any idea of her rage. It was as if she was an afterthought. She would rarely initiate discussions, and usually revealed little about herself, her likes and her dislikes. Any interaction depended upon others starting them. They would be pleasantly unproductive. She would act earnest and helpless while group members acted concerned, until they eventually moved on to more rewarding issues. Group accepted and reinforced her "helpless" defense. Once they stopped, this and her other defenses started to crack and she was forced to look at whether she wanted to stay in treatment and face herself.

6. INTERACTIONS OUTSIDE OF THE ACOA GROUP PROVIDE MEMBERS WITH GREAT OPPORTUNITIES FOR PROGRESS DURING GROUP. This goes against traditional group therapy theory. We find that taking advantage of the fellowship approach developed by groups such as AA and Al-Anon is a unique advantage for ACOAs. Talking on the phone, socializing, and helping each other is essential for the recovery of ACOAs. More important than the activities is their reaction to them. Attempting to develop healthy, intimate relationships in the present will naturally reveal the problem areas of the past. It produces valuable material for group.

If the group didn't help Dan when Jerri was in Florida, he wouldn't have felt connected enough to do the work he did. Laura and Nellie buying a house led to a more concrete examination not only of how they related but the conflicted loyalties group members had. Ranging from Nora trying to formalize picking a restaurant to Joel's claim of brainwashing, going out to dinner provided numerous topics for group. These volatile areas provided many opportunities for ACOAs to explore their feelings and reactions.

7. WHEN ACOAS ARE READY TO SUCCESSFULLY COMPLETE TREATMENT, A MINOR REGRESSION TAKES PLACE WHERE THEY MUST REWORK THE MAJOR ISSUES OF TREATMENT IN ORDER TO CONSOLIDATE THEIR RECOVERY. This comes from two sources. First is a fear that with group being over their lives will be empty. Second is a mistaken notion that recovery means an elimination of old problems and defects. These both cause fear. One because the ACOA is afraid the friendships in group will never be replaced and another because the ACOA knows he isn't perfect and is afraid he has graduated under false pretenses.

Keith handled this by withdrawing into his house. He retreated into a safe haven with a never ending series of chores to keep him occupied. These chores were more predictable than the relationships he had with people. Keith's recovery was solid enough that with a little help he could see what he was doing. His relationships with group members, though viewed as a nuisance during this period, gave him the foundation to come past the regression.

After making such enormous progress with her in-laws and with the birth of her child, Kay was scared. Resigning as Chairwoman of the Universe was frightening since it called into question her entire method of operating. Going back to work was an ill-conceived idea devised in secrecy. The drive which had caused so much trouble in the past now re-established itself. It was a tribute to Kay's recovery that when confronted, she was able to take action. It showed not only how far she had come, but how far she had yet to go.

8. RECOVERY FOR ACOAS IS NOT EASY NOR IS IT ASSURED. It is easy to define recovery as self-awareness, self-acceptance, and the ability to relate intimately with others. However, there are many obstacles to attaining recovery. Many of the ACOAs defenses are designed to minimize the hurt of parental alcoholism. Lacking unconditional nurturing, many AOCAs view life as a struggle for external definition. Faced with the unpredictability of parental alcoholism, ACOAs relate primarily defensively in a manner designed to avoid conflict at all costs.

Not all ACOAs recover. For many awareness and relating are too frightening. They do not have the internal resources to deal with the trauma that has been repressed. Others are too fragile for the give and take true intimacy requires. A significant number have moved beyond the classic ACOA syndrome and suffer from other psychiatric disorders. When treating ACOAs a therapist must be careful not to go too far too fast, and also be cautious of entering areas patients do not have the resources to handle.

9. ALL ACOAS ARE DOING THE BEST THEY CAN. Lack of progress does not mean a lack of good will. Even with his defiance, Joel was trying to manage the best he could. Tom was not closed and remote because he wanted to be. Judy

was not bitter about her father because it was fun. All were just trying to get through life with the resources they had.

In one sense, the most we have to offer ACOAs is affirmation. Even if treatment is not appropriate or doesn't work out, it need not be a negative experience. One of the biggest fears ACOAs have can be described as *"If they really knew me they would see how worthless I am."* Therapists know AOCAs. If they are able to convey care and acceptance with that knowledge, they provide a valuable gift. ACOAs will be able to leave treatment realizing they have been known and affirmed. If they are able to stay, they will eventually be able to know and affirm themselves.

Hidden Riches in Perspective

In the book *Tumbleweeds: A Therapist's Guide to Treatment of ACOAs,*[1] I explored how recovery is to be found in community with others. Recovery will be discovered in the attempt to develop healthy, intimate relationships with other ACOAs in a group setting. These relationships will be based on honesty and vulnerability,and by expressing emotions, identifying needs, and setting limits. Being in community with others enables an ACOA to gain insight into himself and develop self-love and caring as a result of experiencing the love and caring of others.

During the course of these relationships it is inevitable that the trauma and repressed emotions which come from being raised by active alcoholics will give rise to difficulties and emotional responses that are out of proportion to a particular situation. It is important to acknowledge that ACOAs must address and resolve the past. ACOAs are often concerned that if they don't consciously attempt to resolve the pain of their childhoods through activities and exercises, it will never come up. They need not worry. The scars of the past, though often disguised, reveal themselves daily in an ACOA's approach to life, himself, and others. That is why a community of recovering ACOAs is so important. It provides a fertile ground where these problems can arise naturally, and be exposed, explored, and resolved. In *Tumbleweeds* I proposed that the pain of the past is best addressed as a by-product of developing and maintaining healthy, intimate relationships in the present. This results in an increased vulnerability and a decreased sense of self-sufficiency. ACOAs were asked to open themselves to each other and to allow their lives to be revealed as a part of a shared process instead of viewing recovery as a solitary attempt at self-adjustment based on intellectual information.

---

[1] Continuum, 1991.

In my second book *Resistance and Recovery for Adult Children of Alcoholics,*[2] I examined the difficulties ACOAs encounter in the recovery process. Most of the difficulties are rooted in the mistaken notion that hard work, great effort, and radical change are necessary. They approach the recovery process with a sense of apprehension, fear, and sense of impending failure. Healthy families develop the notion that things improve as time progresses. There will be rough spots, but honesty, openness, and shared efforts will enable these problems to be turned into opportunities for further growth. Alcoholic families view the future with dread. Life requires hard work in order for the members to rise above, or at least manage, the downward spiral of alcoholism. Most of their defenses and energies are spent attempting to prevent despair and the perceived looming collapse both of themselves and the world around them. It is no wonder that ACOAs cannot view resistance as natural and valuable to the recovery process. Instead they tend to see it as something to hide and to overcome through hard work.

AOCAs believe they have to **do** a lot of things and **change** a great deal if they are to recover. Recovery is viewed as yet another task that ACOAs must complete. They strive to address issues; they work on character defects; they struggle to share their emotions; and they desperately try to make life better than it was for them when they were growing up. The root of their struggle is the fundamental belief that they are not lovable in and of themselves. ACOAs develop a defensive system based on internal denial of their pain and sense of loss along with external self-censorship. It protects them from the pain of what they reveal to others and prevents others from discovering their weakness and desperation.

Resistance and Recovery claimed that the only task necessary for an ACOA's recovery is to see himself as he actually is and to embrace that vision. The task of the therapy or self-help group is to provide the ACOA with acceptance, love, and caring until he can accept, love, and care for himself. In one sense the majority of years spent in the recovery process are devoted to fighting this surrender and acceptance. The ACOA engages in a solitary, self-directed struggle to change what he would like, avoid what he doesn't want to change, and resist in silent desperation the surrender which is called for. This impossible, hopeless battle to achieve self-worth and self-love through performance and self-directed change will hopefully cause enough frustration and pain that the

---

[2]Continuum, 1991.

ACOA will be forced to allow surrender to occur. Unfortunately, at this moment many leave the recovery process because it is too threatening.

The main point is that **things do not have to change in order for recovery to occur. Recovery occurs and then change happens.** Recovery is defined as a vision of true awareness in which the ACOA sees and accepts himself as he truly is and allows others into his life in openness and vulnerability. The groundwork for this recovery is based on two parts. First is his frustration and weariness with the struggle for self-sufficient change. Second, and most important, is the long-term insistent invitation of his fellow ACOAs to join them in a community of caring and acceptance. Here is that mysticism I talked about. Why was he able to accept their invitation? Why was he able to leave the battle field? I truly don't know. My opinion is that an unexplainable spiritual phenomenom took place. I know it's not very scientific, but I can't come to any other conclusion.

ACOAs are unaware of the richness of life. Their syndrome is based on a strong denial and repression. Although they were necessary to get through the pain of parental alcoholism during their formative years, these defenses have become entrenched, creating a narrow, rigid focus of life and a method of operating based on reaction rather than affirmative action. Perceptions, views, and insights are limited to fit into well-defined, limited structures in order not to threaten their defenses. Instead of seeking to embrace life, they operate to prevent life from squashing them. Their illness forces them to live life with such internal restrictions that they become closed, not only to themselves but also to the world around them. They automatically run each life experience through a psychological strainer that prevents all but the most palatable from being brought to light. Unfortunately, this psychological strainer in addition to being very effective is also non-discriminating. It blocks not only pain, fear, and anger, but joy, happiness, and excitement as well.

The seeds of recovery are to be found in every instant. Recovery is not to be found in therapy rooms or in self-help meetings. **Recovery is life.** All of it! ACOA therapy helps a person to see and realize what has been there all along. Everything changes, but nothing has changed. An ACOA now brings to life a new vision. The blind can now see.